FIRE ENGINES

FROM AROUND THE WORLD

FIRE ENGINES

FROM AROUND THE WORLD

**An illustrated A–Z of contemporary and historical
fire engine manufacturers, coach builders and
special appliance makers, with 375 photographs**

NEIL WALLINGTON

southwater

This edition is published by Southwater, an imprint of Anness Publishing Ltd, Hermes House, 88–89 Blackfriars Road, London SE1 8HA
tel. 020 7401 2077; fax 020 7633 9499
www.southwaterbooks.com; www.annesspublishing.com

If you like the images in this book and would like to investigate using them for publishing, promotions or advertising, please visit our website www.practicalpictures.com for more information.

UK agent: The Manning Partnership Ltd
tel. 01225 478444; fax 01225 478440

UK distributor: Grantham Book Services Ltd
tel. 01476 541080; fax 01476 541061

North American agent/distributor:
National Book Network
tel. 301 459 3366; fax 301 429 5746

Australian agent/distributor:
Pan Macmillan Australia
tel. 1300 135 113; fax 1300 135 103

New Zealand agent/distributor:
David Bateman Ltd
tel. (09) 415 7664; fax (09) 415 8892

Publisher: Joanna Lorenz
Editorial Director: Helen Sudell
Project Editor: Simona Hill
Designer: Mike Morey
Production Controller: Claire Rae

ETHICAL TRADING POLICY
Because of our ongoing ecological investment programme, you, as our customer, can have the pleasure and reassurance of knowing that a tree is being cultivated on your behalf to naturally replace the materials used to make the book you are holding. For further information about this scheme, go to www.annesspublishing.com/trees

Previously published as part of a larger volume, *The World Encyclopedia of Fire Engines and Firefighting*

Acknowledgements
The author wishes to thank the following for their assistance and technical advice during the preparation of this book: Ron Bentley, Eric Billingham, Gary Chapman, Maurice Cole, Detlef Gerth, Mike Hebbard, Andrew Henry, Jerry Hepworth, Chris Jackson, Simon Rowley, S W Stevens-Stratten, Keith Wardell. Thanks to the Chief Officers and uniformed personnel, including photographers of many fire brigades including: British Airports Authority, Cheshire, Cleveland (UK), Cornwall, Devon, Dorset, Essex, Greater Manchester, Hampshire, Humberside, Kent, Lancashire, Leicestershire, Lincolnshire, London, Mid and West Wales, New Orleans (Captain Chis Mickel), Wiltshire, West Midlands Fire Service (Edward Ockenden) and West Yorkshire Fire Service (Brian Saville and Andrew Henson). Eurotunnel, The UK Fire Protection Association, and a number of fire engine manufacturers listed in the book. The librarians of the London Fire Brigade Library and the Fire Service College Library, England. Simona Hill of Anness Publishing for all her hard work and editorial guidance. And lastly my wife Susie, who has given unstinting amounts of practical help and encouragement throughout the marathon compilation of this book.

The publishers would like to thank the following for their generous assistance: Shane Mackichan, Andrew Henry, Shaun Ryan, Steven Schueler and Jerry Sires.

Picture Credits

The publishers would like to thank the following for their kind permission to reproduce their photographs:
Andrew Henry 17, 18 top, 22 top and bottom, 27 bottom, 28 top and bottom right, 32 top, 34 top, 37 top and centre right, 41 top, 44 bottom left, 60 top, 63 top and top centre right, 68 top, 70 bottom, 82 centre and bottom right, 84 bottom and bottom centre, 86 centre, 89 centre and bottom, 90 bottom, 92 centre, 95 top, 110 both, 115 top and centre, 116 centre and bottom, 117 bottom, 118 bottom and 127 centre.
Bob Dubbert 87 top, 22 centre, 35 centre, 61 bottom, 66 top centre, 77 bottom, 86 bottom, 106 centre and bottom, 113 centre and 123 second from bottom.
Dan Goyer 12 bottom, 13 centre right, 38 centre, 39 bottom, 58 bottom, 59 bottom, 61 bottom, 86 top, 92 bottom, 93 bottom, 107 top, 109 top right and bottom, 111 bottom, 115 bottom and 124 top.
Dave Stewardson 28 bottom left, 30 bottom, 31, 42 centre, 46 top and bottom, 47 top, 51 top, second from top and bottom right, 53 top, 60 centre, 73 bottom and bottom centre, 75 top, 87 top and bottom, 88 bottom, 89 top, 98 bottom, 99 centre, 106 top, 108 top, 112 bottom, 120 centre and 125 bottom.
Iveco 63 bottom three pictures.
Jerry Hepworth 8 bottom, 9 top, 11 top, 25 top and bottom, 29 centre, 34 bottom right, 52 top, 71 bottom and bottom centre, 79 second from bottom, 81 bottom and 102 bottom.
Jerry Sires 12 centre, 36 centre and bottom, 38 top, 41 bottom, 42 top and bottom, 49 top and centre, 53 bottom, 54 bottom, 55 top and bottom, 57 top, centre and bottom, 62 top and second from top, 65 bottom, 67 top, centre and bottom, 73 top and top centre, 74 top and bottom, 87 centre, 90 centre, 94 all, 99 bottom, 102 top, 108 centre, 113 bottom, 116 bottom and 121 top.
Keith Wardell 8 top, 11 centre, 14 centre right and centre left, 19 top right, 26 top, 29 bottom left and bottom right, 33 top, 35 top, 40 top, 43 top, centre and bottom, 44 centre right and bottom right, 45 top left and centre right, 80 top right, 62 bottom right, 68 bottom left and second from bottom left, 69 bottom, 70 centre, 71 top and top centre, 76 top centre, top right and centre, 77 centre, 78 bottom, 79 top left, 80 bottom left, 81 top and centre, 85 top and centre, 91 centre, 92 bottom, 93 top left, 96 bottom, 97 bottom, 119 top, 120 top and 127 top right.
National Motor Museum 44 centre left and 97 top.
Neil Wallington 11 bottom, 14 top and bottom, 18 bottom, 19 second from bottom and bottom, 26 bottom, 33 centre and bottom, 34 bottom left, 37 centre left and bottom, 40 bottom, 52 centre, 59 bottom centre, 68 bottom left, 70 top, 75 top centre right and top centre left, 76 bottom, 77 top, 78 bottom

centre, 79 top right, 80 top, 83 right, 91 top and bottom, 93 top right, 95 bottom left, 100 all, 102 centre, 103 top right, 120 bottom, 126 bottom and 127 top left.
Roger Mardon 114.
Shane Mackichan 13 centre top, 20 all, 21 centre and bottom, 24, 27 top and top centre, 30 top and third from top, 38 bottom, 39 top and bottom, 45 second from bottom, 48 top and centre, 50 top left, 51 bottom left, 52 bottom, 53 centre, 54 top, 55 centre, 58 top and centre, 59 top and top centre left, 61 top, second from top and third from top, 62 bottom left, 66 bottom, 74 centre, 75 bottom, 84 top and top centre right, 85 bottom, 88 top, 99 top, 108 bottom, 112 top and centre, 122 top, 123 top and bottom, 124 centre, bottom left and bottom right, 125 top and centre.
Shaun Ryan 9 centre and bottom, 12 top, 23 top and bottom, 27 second from bottom, 30 second from top, 32 top, 35 bottom, 36 top, 45 top and second from top, 48 bottom, 50 centre and bottom, 56 top and bottom, 59 top centre right, 60 bottom, 78 top and second from top, 90 top, 98 top, 103 bottom, 107 bottom, 109 top left and centre, 111 top, 113 top, 121 centre, 122 centre and bottom, 123 second from top and 126 top.
Simon Rowley 78 second from bottom and 95 bottom right.
Steven Schueler 10 bottom, 15 (all), 16 (all), 47 bottom, 65 top and centre, 72 top, centre and bottom, 82 top and top centre right, 83 left, 104 all, 105 all, 118 top.
S W Stevens-Stratten 8 centre, 10 top, 19 top left, 25 centre, 29 top left, 34 top centre, 69 centre, 80 bottom right, 96 top and 101 top,
Terry Yip 13 top and bottom, 45 bottom, 49 bottom, 66 top and 88 centre.
TRH 29 top right, 32 centre, 44 top, 69 top, 79 bottom, 82 bottom left, 101 centre and bottom, 103 top left and 119 centre and bottom.

Note

In describing various fire engines throughout this book, a fire engine may be described, for example, as a 1990 Dennis F127/Saxon/Simon ST240 24m/78ft aerial platform ladder. The first reference (a Dennis F127) refers to the make of the fire engine's chassis/cab; the second to the bodybuilding company; and the third reference is to the manufacturer of the aerial ladder assembly and mechanism fitted.

The alphabetic A–Z listing includes a few companies that actually build a complete fire engine, those that supply the chassis/cab element, and a number that construct the bodywork and firefighting/rescue fitments and equipment, to the specification of the fire brigade concerned.

The listing also includes a number of companies that have long since disappeared from the scene but have clearly made an important contribution to fire engine design and development over the years.

CONTENTS

INTRODUCTION

The world's major fire engine manufacturers past and present are identified in this book. It would be impossible to include every manufacturer that has ever existed, but here is a sample of those that have shaped the design and engineering of the modern fire engine, whether it is a pumper, aerial ladder or specialist rescue tender.

The book also illustrates something of the design development over the years. Today, few fire engine manufacturers produce a complete fire and rescue vehicle. Most brigades select a suitably modified commercial chassis/cab upon which a specialist bodybuilding company designs and fabricates the bodywork, together with fire engineering and other fittings necessary for a particular operational use.

■ OPPOSITE *This 1994 Volvo FL10/Angloco/Metz DLK 30m/ 98.4ft turntable ladder of Hampshire Fire and Rescue Service, England, negotiates a low arch leading into Winchester Cathedral.*

■ LEFT *A 2001 International/ Australian Fire Company emergency response/pumper unit of the Australian Fire Service.*

A E C

A major British manufacturer of bus, coach and lorry chassis, the Associated Equipment Company (AEC) began to produce fire engine chassis before World War II, and its fire engines saw front-line service in commonwealth countries for almost 50 years. The AEC Regal, Regent and Mercury chassis were used extensively, in conjunction with several bodybuilders, to produce various fire engines, including pumping engines, or pumps, turntable ladders, hydraulic platforms and emergency tenders. During the later years of production, a range of specials were built, including foam tenders, control units, heavy rescue units and prime movers.

Some early AECs utilized a Meadows 9.5-litre petrol engine, although the heavy-duty Mercury chassis, which first appeared in 1953, was powered by the AEC AV 470 diesel engine. At that time AEC pumps were generally put on the Regent chassis, a popular bus and coach chassis. In the 1960s the TGM, a restyled chassis that incorporated a tilt cab, was introduced, making AEC fire

AEC MERCURY TURNTABLE LADDER	
Year	1965
Engine	AEC AV 470 diesel
Power	9.6-litre
Transmission	5-speed manual
Features	Merryweather ladder

■ ABOVE *This 1952 AEC Regent/ Merryweather pump escape served in Wales.*

■ BELOW *A wooden extension ladder formed part of the equipment of this 1966 AEC Mercury/Merryweather foam tender.*

■ ABOVE *A 1967 AEC Marquis Seven pump before delivery to Leicester City Fire Brigade, England.*

engines among the first fire service vehicles to have this innovative facility.

AEC is probably best remembered in the fire engine arena for being fitted with various turntable ladders and hydraulic platforms. Merryweather turntable ladders consisted of four steel sections with a maximum 30m/100ft extension. Early AEC/Merryweather turntable ladders utilized a power take-off to drive mechanically the various evolutions of the ladder, along with a manual jacking system. Merryweather introduced hydraulic power to its turntable ladders in 1957, enabling the operator to sit at a rear-mounted control console on the rotating turntable turret. The jacking system was also hydraulically powered. Later AEC turntable ladder vehicles incorporated a 1,600-litres/350-gallons-per-minute

■ RIGHT *A 1965 AEC Mercury/HCB Angus/Simon SS70 hydraulic platform belonging to Lincolnshire Fire Brigade, England, stands at the ready.*

pump to supply an independent firefighting water supply when the ladder was in use as a water tower.

The first hydraulic platform to be built on an AEC chassis arrived at Glasgow Fire Service, in Scotland, in 1960. It utilized a set of Simon SS model booms to provide a maximum working height of 20m/65ft and was one of a new breed of aerial fire engines that inspired the steady development and wider use of hydraulic platforms by the fire service.

Pumping fire engines using the AEC Regent chassis were used by a variety of bodybuilders to suit the needs of particular fire brigades. In 1961, for

instance, London Fire Brigade introduced 11 dual-purpose Marquis pumps bodied by both Merryweather and Carmichael. In service these engines could be configured to run either as pump escapes (carrying a 15m/50ft wheeled escape ladder) or simply as pumps with a 10m/35ft extension ladder.

Rear or transverse high-output pump options were available on AEC fire engines, usually with an integral 450-litre/100-gallon water tank.

AEC became part of the Leyland conglomerate in 1962 and by the early 1970s the AEC name had ceased to appear on fire engines.

AHRENS-FOX

Founded in 1908, in Cincinnati, USA, Ahrens-Fox was one of the earliest American manufacturers of motorized fire engines. It built a petrol-engine pumper in 1911 and devised its first aerial ladder in 1923.

Ahrens-Fox fire engines had a reputation for being extremely well engineered and they carried front-mounted pumps with prominent capacious air vessels. In the late 1930s the company produced some innovative,

■ RIGHT *A front-mounted pump and air vessel are typical features of the 1928 Ahrens-Fox NS4 pumper.*

semi-streamlined enclosed-cab pumpers. Although it went into liquidation in 1936, it continued to build fire engines to special order for many more years during which several

commercial rescue attempts were made. The company was eventually acquired by Mack before it disappeared altogether from the American fire and rescue scene in the late 1950s.

■ LEFT *This 1950 HT 4,500-litres/1,000-gallons-per-minute pumper was the pinnacle of Ahrens-Fox technical achievement.*

M-TYPE PUMPER	
Year	1927
Engine	6-cylinder petrol
Power	55hp
Transmission	4-speed manual
Features	4-cylinder fire pump

ALBION

■ LEFT *An Albion pump, c.1935, built with an unusual forward control cab arrangement. Note the top-mounted hose reel drum.*

The Albion Motor Car Company first built fire engines at its factory in Glasgow, Scotland, in 1903. These early models, based on the Albion car chassis of that time, were designed as hose cars, sometimes with a chemical engine to provide a basic hose reel water supply. The company was one of the first

FT PUMP	
Year	1928
Engine	4-cylinder petrol
Power	70bhp
Transmission	4-speed manual
Features	Braidwood body

manufacturers, in the 1920s, to use a shaft drive to the rear wheels. Over the next 50 years Albions went into service in several British fire brigades, mostly as pumps, and a number were supplied to countries as far away as Australia. Albion continued to build fire engines for use in Britain after World War II. Including water tenders or dual-purpose pumps, emergency tenders, foam

tenders and salvage units, these engines utilized the Albion CX/Chieftain/Claymore and Clydesdale chassis fitted mostly with 6.5-litre Leyland diesel engines, often with Carmichael bodywork.

By 1972, when Albion became part of the Leyland Motors Group, it had faded from the fire engine scene, although several of its fire engines remained in active service until 1988.

ALEXANDER PERRIE

Based in New South Wales, Australia, Alexander Perrie has manufactured several hundred fire engines of various types for operational service in the New South Wales Brigade and the Northern Territory Fire Brigades, as well as for the Australian military services.

Typical of the Alexander Perrie pumpers of the 1970s and 1980s were the batch built on International 1810D chassis for New South Wales Fire Brigade. These were fitted with a Godiva 3,400 litres/750 gallons per minute rear-mounted pump and a 1,800-litre/400-gallon water tank. A number of this series of pumpers were configured to carry hydraulic rescue equipment.

More recently, the company has completed the fitting out of a specialized breathing apparatus and response semi-trailer unit, again for New South Wales Fire Brigade. This fire engine is drawn by a Mercedes Actros 2643 6x4 with

430hp engine and 15-speed transmission. The tractor has a sleeper cabin, and the trailer has a fully integrated and air-conditioned fibreglass body, a three-phase 240-volt power supply and cylinder-recharging equipment. Ergonomic stowage for a full range of hazmat gear including

■ ABOVE *Fitted with rear-mounted Godiva 3,400-litres/750-gallons-per-minute pump and 1,800-litre/400-gallon tank, this 1986 pumper also carries rescue equipment.*

protective suits allows for easy access and lifting down. The unit also has a training area and a striking external colour and signage scheme.

ALFRED MILES

■ RIGHT *This 1950 Commer QX/Alfred Miles emergency tender once served in Bootle, England.*

This bodybuilding company was based in Cheltenham, England, and in the post-World War II period bodied a number of water tenders for rural fire brigades in the UK. Much of the work was based on Commer and Bedford chassis and adopted a style involving folding doors to the rear crew compartment, two transverse lockers and a low-level hose reel on each side of the fire engine. A rear-mounted 2,270-litres/500-gallons-per-minute pump was fed by an 1,800-litre/400-gallon water tank. Alfred Miles water tenders could be adapted for dual-purpose use, carrying either a 10m/35ft extension ladder or a 15m/50ft wheeled escape ladder.

■ LEFT *This Dennis F8/Alfred Miles water tender was produced in 1952.*

COMMER QX WATER TENDER	
Year	1954
Engine	3-cylinder 2-stroke diesel
Power	4.75-litre
Transmission	4-speed manual
Features	folding doors to rear cab

ALVIS

Having successfully produced a number of military vehicles and armoured cars through the 1920s and 1930s, Alvis Ltd of Coventry, England, developed this activity to embrace the manufacture of a number of airfield fire and rescue vehicles. These included powerful foam and crash tenders, all with 6x6 cross-country capability. A 1959 Alvis fire engine was built as an amphibious airfield fire tender for the Royal Ceylon Air Force. Like most of the Alvis range, it was powered by a Rolls-Royce B81

240bhp, 6-cylinder engine, with foam equipment supplied by the Pyrene company. Many Alvis 6x6 airfield foam tenders went into service with the Royal Air Force Fire Service in the 1950s.

■ BELOW *Over 80 1954 model 6x6 Alvis/Pyrene military airfield crash tenders were delivered to Britain's Royal Air Force during the 1950s.*

ALVIS/PYRENE MK 6 CRASH TENDER	
Year	1954
Engine	R-R B81 8-cylinder petrol
Power	240bhp
Transmission	manual preselector
Features	Salamander chassis style

AMERICAN LAFRANCE

American LaFrance was formed in 1903 from mergers of various earlier fire engine builders, one of which was the LaFrance Company, originally founded in 1873 as a steam engine manufacturer.

At first the company produced only horse-drawn steam pumps, but in 1910 it built its first petrol-powered fire vehicle in the form of a combination hose car.

By 1916 the company had a catalogue of motor-driven models, the most powerful of which was a pumper with a firefighting water output of 4,500 litres/1,000 gallons per minute. The pumpers were developed over the next two decades and the arrival of the V12 240hp engine in 1931 allowed for even greater pumping capacity. With high-rise buildings getting taller in the USA, American LaFrance produced a super pumper, in 1937, that could output 13,500 litres/3,000 gallons per minute.

In 1929, American LaFrance was the first manufacturer to provide all-wheel braking. Towards the end of World War II, it introduced an innovative forward-control all-enclosed cab. Powered by an American LaFrance V12 petrol engine

■ LEFT *Gridley Fire Department in California, USA, formerly owned this preserved 1926 American LaFrance pumper.*

■ LEFT *Cranston Heights Fire Company, USA, owned this white 1931 pumper.*

■ BELOW LEFT *This 2002 FL80 pumper/aerial ladder was delivered to British Columbia, Canada.*

and with a 6,750-litre/1,500-gallon fire pump, this vehicle soon set the standard in American pumping fire engines.

In 1973 the company introduced custom-built pumpers, a number of which went into service with the New

York Fire Department. With an empty vehicle weight of 10.2 tons, the range came with a five-man cab and a Detroit Diesel V6 350hp power unit driving through an Allison automatic transmission. All were available with pump capacity options of 4,500–9,000 litres/1,000–2,000 gallons per minute. The company also built the Challenger and Conquest pumper models on other makes of chassis.

From its earliest days American LaFrance was an innovative builder of aerial ladders, and by World War II had supplied over 1,500 aerial fire engines.

In 1966 American LaFrance became part of the corporation known as A-T-O Inc, which owned the Snorkel Fire Equipment Company. The merger led to a range of American LaFrance rear and centre-mounted aerial ladders with telescopic sections and booms that combined the operational attributes of the original products of both companies.

ANDERSON'S ENGINEERING

Based at Langley, British Columbia, near Vancouver, Canada, Anderson's Engineering Ltd was formed in 1972 for the manufacture of custom-built fire engines. The company soon earned a reputation as a quality bodybuilder, able to supply a range of reliable pumpers, mini-pumpers, tankers, aerial ladders and platforms, rescue units, and various other tenders.

Anderson's early sales were to western Canadian fire brigades but their fire engines soon started to appear right across Canada and then overseas in countries such as Chile, Saudi Arabia, Guam and Indonesia. By the early 1980s Anderson's fire trucks were also being purchased by several American fire departments.

In 1986, Bronto Skylift entered into an agreement to allow Anderson to mount the Bronto aerial platform ladder range on various commercial chassis with Anderson bodywork. The first of these Anderson/Bronto aerials were mounted on International chassis. Later five Bronto 52m/170ft aerials mounted on Pacific 4-axle chassis were delivered to Montreal Fire Brigade. At the time, these were the tallest aerials anywhere in North America.

■ LEFT *Far from its Canadian place of manufacture, this 1995 Anderson Western Star 4x4 pumper provides firefighting and rescue cover at the Placer Dome Mine, in Zaldivar, Chile.*

■ BELOW LEFT *Sidney Fire Department, in British Columbia, Canada, run this 1994 FL80 Anderson long-wheelbase pumper. This fire engine carries a 2,270-litre/500-gallon water tank and has an output of 4,725 litres/1,045 gallons per minute.*

■ RIGHT *Designed for use in petrochemical installations, this 1982 Anderson foam tender is seen here in service at Shell Oil's Shellburn Refinery, Burnaby, British Columbia, Canada.*

■ BELOW *A 1994 Anderson/Duplex 6x4 33m/110ft rear-mount aerial ladder incorporates a considerable amount of equipment storage space.*

Following the acquisition of Bronto in 1995 by the group that owned Emergency One, Anderson's forged a new alliance with Smeal to mount and body its aerial ladders, subsequently delivering a number of these fire engines across Canada. However, despite a successful 28-year trading period, Anderson's suffered financially in early 2000, and they never recovered. The company finally closed its fire engine plant in November of the same year.

ANGLOCO

For more than 25 years this independent company, based in Yorkshire, England, has designed and manufactured a range of specialist firefighting vehicles for a large number of British and overseas fire brigades, including many in the Middle East, the Caribbean and Africa. Built on a number of commercial chassis, including Scania, DAF, Mercedes and Land Rover, Angloco's fire engines range from basic water tenders through to high-rise Bronto aerial ladder platforms. In addition to being a significant supplier to the British fire service, Angloco currently manufactures fire engines for 38 countries. Recent export orders have included water/foam tenders to Kenya and Guyana, a Scania/Bronto F32 aerial ladder platform to Barbados,

a Scania control unit to Bahrain, and a DAF 11,000-litre/2,420-gallon water tender to Mauritus.

■ ABOVE *This 1990 Volvo FL10/Angloco/Bronto 33m/108ft-aerial ladder platform is in service with London Fire Brigade.*

■ RIGHT *A 1990 Leyland 180/Angloco water tender stands ready for action.*

AUSTIN

Already well established as a major British car and commercial vehicle manufacturer in the 1930s, Austin entered the fire engine scene in a big way in 1939. With war clouds gathering over Europe, it produced large numbers of government utility fire engines for the wartime auxiliary fire service, subsequently known as the National Fire Service. The two chassis cab models involved were the K2 and K4. The 2 or 3-ton/2,036 or 3,054kg K2 version came as a towing vehicle designed to carry a five-man crew and pull a trailer pump. The larger 5-ton/5,090kg K4 model was built either as a five-man crew heavy pump capable of delivering 2,270 litres/ 500 gallons of water per minute, or as a hand-operated 18m/60ft turntable ladder. The steel K4 turntable ladder consisted of three extending sections made by Merryweather. These fire

engines carried a crew of three and some were also fitted with front-mounted pumps. A number of all these wartime versions survived into post-war operational service with many being

■ LEFT *This 1959 HCB/Angus bodied Austin FFK foam/salvage tender remained operational until 1974. It carried an aluminium extension ladder, roof-mounted searchlights and amber warning lights.*

retired only in the 1960s, and a few have been preserved in working order in the UK. In 1959, Austin produced their 4x4 jeep-style Gipsy chassis, which a number of rural fire brigades used as a lightweight fire engine.

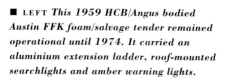

■ LEFT *An ex-wartime National Fire Service Austin K4 heavy pump unit fitted with a 15m/50ft wheeled escape ladder is seen here in service in the 1950s.*

AUSTRAL

While it was in existence, this Australian enterprise constructed a number of fire engines for the domestic market. These were built either on Austral's own chassis designs or those of various commercial manufacturers.

Austral's principal fire chassis was the Firepac, which came in two versions – the smaller 3000 and the heavier 4000. The pumper versions of these two models were constructed with Caterpillar turbocharged diesel engines, automatic transmission and Rosenbauer pumps. They also had air suspension as a standard feature. A number of Firepacs went into service in the states of Queensland and New South Wales. In the latter, they were also used operationally as hazardous material and rescue/salvage tenders.

■ LEFT *The Caterpillar 3116 turbocharged diesel engine of this Firepac 3000 series fire engine is incorporated into the general Firepac features of automatic transmission, integral frame and air suspension. The vehicle's Rosenbauer NH30 pump can be either midship or rear-mounted.*

■ BELOW *Some Austral fire appliances were built on proprietary chassis. This is one of two identical aerials, the only two of this type in Australia, built with a Simon ALP340 40m/130ft platform on a Scania P113H 8x4 chassis.*

■ ABOVE *In 1996, New South Wales took delivery of four pumpless Firepacs, built on a slightly longer than standard wheelbase and with a powerful diesel engine. They were painted in experimental colours.*

In addition to pumpers, Austral manufactured a number of aerials for the Australian market. Among these were two Simon 40m/130ft aerial ladder

platforms mounted on a Scania P113H-360, 8x4 chassis. This unique pair of vehicles was delivered to the fire department of Queensland.

When Austral was acquired by Varley in the late 1990s, the Firepac model was used as a basis for further development and it eventually reappeared as the 4-door Varley Commander.

AUSTRALIAN FIRE COMPANY

The origins of this Australian company go back to the dissolution of the Carey Gulley Engineering firm. The newly formed, privately owned Australian Fire Company initially took over the existing factory site before moving to its own headquarters base in Gepps Cross, South Australia.

The range of Australian Fire Company fire engines included small quick attack pumpers, heavy-duty pumpers, aerials and rescue tenders. Imported fire equipment included pumps from WS Darley, and aerial ladders from Metz, Snorkel and Bronto.

The company's fire engines are in service across Australia. The range includes the largest fleet of Freightliner fire engines, used by the Melbourne brigade. Other chassis used include the Scania G94 series, in various pumper guises in New South Wales and Canberra. In 1998 a Scania 113H with a Bronto F37HDT aerial ladder platform was delivered to Melbourne.

During 1998–99, the company fulfilled a contract for 26 crash tenders built on Emergency One HPR 4x4 chassis for the Australian military. Delivered in kit form, these were assembled with an Australian Fire Company aluminium body.

In 2000, the company, along with its designs and manufacturing styles, was acquired by the Skilled Equipment Manufacturing Company.

■ RIGHT *Transfield Fire Service provides contracted fire protection to the Royal Australian Air Force. The Edinburgh base, in South Australia, has two of these Category 4 units in service to complement the Austral Crash Fire Rescue units also stationed there. Firefighting equipment consists of a Hatz/Darley pump, a 2,500-litre/550-gallon water tank, a 300-litre/66-gallon foam tank and a Feecon monitor.*

■ LEFT *Australian Fire Company's first 4-Series Scania fire appliance was delivered in 1998 to the Australian Capital Territory Fire Brigade.*

■ ABOVE *Victoria's Country Fire Authority has a trio of Telesquirt appliances in service. This Frankston-based 1998 example is typical, with a 5,000 litres/1,000 gallons per minute Darley pump and 1,800-litre/400-gallon water tank.*

AVIA

After World War II, a number of Czechoslovakian pumping fire engines were built on the locally produced Avia chassis. Many of these were configured as light pumps, using the A30 2.68m/105in short wheelbase chassis powered by a 80bhp diesel engine. These were unusual in having an eight-man crew cab on a light fire engine, with

LIGHT PUMP

Year	1965
Engine	4-cylinder petrol
Power	80bhp
Transmission	4-speed manual
Features	7-man crew cab

a weight of a little over 5 tons. These lightweight fire engines carried a portable fire pump, a short extension ladder and a modest range of firefighting equipment.

■ ABOVE *This Deutz/Avia light pumping unit is pictured in service in the Spanish resort of Mallorca.*

OTHER MAKES

■ ALEXIS FIRE EQUIPMENT COMPANY

The Alexis Fire Equipment Company was founded in America in 1947 after vehicle repairer Gene Morris decided that he could build a better-quality truck than some of those he repaired: thus his fire engine company was born.

Since then Alexis has experienced tremendous growth and expansion and nowadays operates from a headquarters site at Alexis, Illinois. The company offers a wide range of fire engines, including pumpers and aerial ladders available on either 4x4 or 6x4 chassis, heavy rescue and mini-rescue units, and a range of water tankers.

■ AMERICAN FIRE ENGINE COMPANY

The American Fire Engine Company had its origins in Seneca Falls, Elmira, New York State, in 1891, and in 1900 amalgamated with four other significant

independent manufacturers of manual and steam pumping fire engines (Ahrens, Button, Clapp & Thomas, and Silsby) to form the International Fire Engine Company. In 1903 it changed its name to American LaFrance Fire Engine Company.

■ AMOSKEAG

The Amoskeag Manufacturing Company of Manchester, New Hampshire, USA, was one of the first American builders of steam-driven pumpers, and its fire engines were in service in New York as early as 1860. It quickly became one of the more successful American manufacturers, supplying a large number of steam pumpers to some of the largest city fire departments from coast to coast. In 1863 Amoskeag took two of its latest models to the Crystal Palace Fire Engine Trials in London, England. American steamers tended to be more heavily engineered than British versions and both performed impressively.

In 1876, Amoskeag built the first successful self-propelled steam fire engine and thereafter continued to develop this type of vehicle, constructing a number of huge and technically advanced engines. The rear-driven axle of some later Amoskeag steamers incorporated a differential to help maneouvre the heavy vehicle round tight corners.

One of these giant steamers, thought to be the world's largest fire engine at the time, was delivered in 1894 to Hartford Fire Department, in Connecticut, USA. It weighed just over 7 tons and, thanks to a double chain drive from the steam engine, could travel at up to 50kmh/30mph. However, as the monster was reputed to be very difficult to steer and stop, its speed was limited to a less potentially dangerous 20kmh/12mph. This giant fire engine could pump a jet of water over an impressive distance of 105m/350ft. It was claimed to be the world's most powerful fire pump of its day.

BARIBBI

Until the early 1980s, most fire engines used in Italy were built by the Baribbi company. For their standard Italian water tenders, Baribbi utilized the 4-ton OM/Fiat 150 chassis fitted with a high- and low-pressure pump with a capacity of up to 1,700 litres/375 gallons per minute and a 3,000-litre/660-gallon

AIRPORT FOAM TENDER	
Year	1974
Engine	V8 diesel
Power	300bhp
Transmission	manual
Features	6x6

water tank. Baribbi also used the OM chassis for a number of rural service water tankers and airport foam/crash tenders. Some of their larger airport fire engines use a heavyweight 6x6 OM/Fiat chassis to carry an 11,000-litre/2,420-gallon water tank and 1,500 litres/

■ ABOVE *A c.1992 Scania/Baribbi emergency tender showing locker space and use of the roof for equipment storage.*

330 gallons of foam concentrate. These Squalo (Shark) series vehicles have an all-up operational weight of just over 32 tons and are provided with a tilt cab.

■ BELOW *Horsham Fire Brigade, England, ran this c.1934 Bedford pump.*

BEDFORD

By the early 1930s Bedford was producing several chassis suitable for fire brigade use at the Vauxhall Motors plant in Luton, England. A number of the smallest of these, a 2-ton/2,030kg truck chassis with a 3.2-litre, 6-cylinder petrol engine, had gone into service as pumping fire engines or hose carriers.

After World War II, Bedford chassis were used extensively for British fire engines as both pumps and turntable ladders, and a number were being exported to other countries. The 5- and 7-ton S and SB models were particularly popular during the early 1950s. Birmingham Fire & Ambulance Service set the standard when they commissioned 27 pump escapes built on the 3.2m/126in shortened SB coach chassis. This ran with a 15m/50ft wheeled escape ladder, a 450-litre/100-gallon water tank and a 2,270-litres/500-gallons-per-minute water pump.

■ BELOW *Peterborough Volunteer Fire Brigade, one of the oldest volunteer brigades in Britain, originally ran this late 1960s Bedford R series 4x4 pump.*

■ ABOVE *This 1951 Bedford pump escape was built on a shortened SB chassis.*

■ BELOW *1960s Bedford fire engines – a 1962 Magirus turntable ladder, a pump and a hose rescue tender – once served in New Zealand.*

■ BOTTOM *Bedford Green Goddess fire engines were commissioned by the British Government in 1953 as reserve pumps.*

BEDFORD TK/HCB ANGUS	
Year	1966
Engine	6-cylinder petrol
Power	176bhp
Transmission	4-speed automatic
Features	Rolls-Royce B61 engine

As part of an expanded civil defence programme, in 1953 the British government ordered hundreds of reserve fire engines for use by the Auxiliary Fire Service that then operated throughout the UK. These pumping and specialist fire engines were built on the Bedford S series chassis and finished in green livery. They used the Bedford 6-cylinder 4.9-litre petrol engine, and were fitted with an 1,800-litre/400-gallon water tank, a 4,500-litre/1,000-gallon pump and a 10m/35ft extension ladder. A significant number of these Green Goddesses, as they came to be known, have survived in an updated form into the twenty-first century for use as reserve fire engines.

During the 1960s and 1970s a wide range of Bedford chassis types, including the B, R, TJ, TK, TKL, TKEL and KGS series among a number of other Bedford models, were being used for hundreds of fire engine applications. These ranged from the 2-ton TJ to a 16-ton version of the TK. Later Bedford fire engines used Perkins and Cummins diesel engines. Although production ceased in 1988, many Bedford fire engines are still in service in various parts of the world.

BICKLE SEAGRAVE/KING SEAGRAVE

This Canadian company's involvement with fire engines dates back to 1906 when R S Bickle began to manufacture hand and horse-drawn chemical carts, before moving on to develop motor-powered fire engines around 1915. In that year, a move to Woodstock, Ontario, saw the founding of the Bickle Fire Engine Company.

In 1923, Bickle made an agreement with the Ahrens-Fox Fire Engine Company of Ohio, USA, to build their fire engines for the Canadian market. For almost ten years, Bickle used Ahrens-Fox chassis and some body parts for their fire engines and these bore the name *The Canadian Ahrens-Fox*. In 1924, the company moved to newer and larger premises in Woodstock and from 1928 began to build customized pumpers around a four-model range. The chassis choice for fire chiefs included Ford, Chevrolet, Packard, and American LaFrance.

Following enquiries from Montreal and Quebec City Fire Departments in the late 1920s for short-wheelbase aerial ladders, RS Bickle came to a commercial arrangement with the Magirus company of Ulm, Germany, a

■ TOP *A 1978 Scot 6x4 Fire King 16.7m/ 55ft Snorkel of Revelstoke Fire Department, British Columbia, with 4,767l/ 1,050gpm midships mounted pump.*

■ ABOVE *This 1966 GMC/King Seagrave pumper has a 2,837 litre/625gpm pump and 2,724-litre/600-gallon water tank.*

■ LEFT *Crowsnest Pass Fire Department, Blairmore, Alberta, run this 1974 Ford C900 6x4 Fire King 26m/85ft Snorkel. It has a 4,767l/1,050 gpm midships pump and 908-litre/200- gallon water tank.*

■ RIGHT *A 1982 International CO 1950B/King pumper of Esquimalt, British Columbia.*

■ BELOW RIGHT *A well preserved 1953 Bickle Seagrave light pump.*

prominent manufacturer of turntable ladders for European brigades. Under this agreement, Bickle imported the Magirus wooden ladder sections and built a number of Bickle/Magirus turntable ladders for Canadian fire brigades. These fire engines became the forerunners of rear-mount aerial ladders in North America. A further alliance in the early 1930s saw Bickle mounting new hydraulically operated wooden ladders built by Peter Pirsch & Sons of Kenosha, Wisconsin, USA.

However, in 1935 came a significant marriage between Bickle and the Seagrave Corporation of Columbus, Ohio, when Bickle took over the production of Seagrave fire engines for the whole of Canada. The name of the enlarged company was changed to Bickle Seagrave Ltd and before long it had become the largest fire engine builder in Canada, with a range that embraced most types of pumpers, rescue tenders and aerial ladders.

Following the death, in 1949, of the company founder, Robert Sydney Bickle the ownership of Bickle Seagrave passed through a number of hands. Following some difficult times, the company eventually ceased trading and closed down in 1956. At this stage, Vernon Bickle King, a nephew of the founder, stepped in. At that time, he had a successful truck and trailer business in Woodstock and purchased the manufacturing rights to the Bickle Seagrave company. Fire engine production resumed in May 1956 under the new name of King Seagrave. A new factory was opened nearby in 1962 and over the next few years, a steady flow of pumpers and hydraulic platforms were built. At the same time King Seagrave became the Canadian agent for American Snorkel aerials. By 1971,

King Seagrave had a successful coast-to-coast operation with 475 employees.

However, with the acquisition of Seagrave by the FWD Corporation in the early 1970s, King Seagrave lost the exclusive right to market Seagrave fire engines in Canada. Recession in the early 1980s brought further difficulties. A change of ownership for the company preceded bankruptcy in 1984 and with

it the end of two company names that between them had built fire engines for a large part of the Canadian fire service for almost 70 years. Mainly serving the domestic market, the company had also exported to several distant countries.

■ BELOW *This 1985 pumper has a 6,810 litres-/1,500 gallons-per-minute pump and 3,405-litre/750-gallon water tank.*

BRIJBASI

With bases in New Delhi and Bombay, Brijbasi Hi-Tech Udyog Ltd manufactures a wide range of lightweight and heavy fire and rescue vehicles, mostly based on suitable Tata

WATER TENDER	
Year	1972
Engine	6-cylinder diesel
Power	180bhp
Transmission	manual
Features	2,270lpm/500gpm pump

and Leyland chassis models. The Brijbasi range includes first-strike units, water tenders, foam tenders and trailer-mounted, high-discharge foam and water monitors for use by various petro-chemical and industrial fire brigades.

■ ABOVE *Adorned with a floral garland, this Brijbasi Udyog Tata 1210 emergency tender belongs to the Delhi Fire Service. It carries breathing apparatus, various rescue tools, as well as a powerful generator for providing emergency lighting.*

BRONTO

For 40 years or more Bronto Skylift Oy Ab has been a leading manufacturer and innovator of high-rise firefighting vehicles, with both aerial ladder platforms and hydraulic platforms. The company, which has its headquarters in Tampere, Finland, was acquired in 1995 by the Federal Signal Corporation of America. Over 5,000 Bronto aerial fire engines can currently be found in operational service with fire brigades in more than 110 countries worldwide.

■ LEFT *A 1997 Emergency One Hurricane/Superior provides the 8x4 base for this 50m/165ft Bronto aerial platform. Belonging to Calgary Fire Department, Canada, it is one of the world's highest platforms.*

Bronto firefighting aerial ladder platforms come in various height ranges from a basic F23 23m/75ft model to the staggering F88 at 88m/290ft, which has

to be mounted on a heavy 5-axle chassis. A popular Bronto is the 28m/92ft aerial ladder platform (the 28-2TI model), which is in service in many city fire brigades and is often found mounted on the Volvo FL10 or the Scania G93M/P113H tandem-axle chassis. Bronto aerials also incorporate add-on features such as lighting, both at the ladder head and for the fireground, camera connections and rescue chutes.

■ LEFT *The Ottawa Fire Department, Canada, runs this 6x4 Pacific/Bronto 40m/130ft aerial platform. The size and complexity of the hydraulic telescopic booms make this an awesome piece of equipment. The operator controls the platform from the cage at the rear end.*

BUFFALO

The Buffalo Fire Appliance Corporation was established in New York in 1895 to produce fire extinguishers and similar equipment. In 1922, the company built its first fire engine and from then on manufactured a range of pumpers, chemical trucks, and ladder trucks based on various commercial chassis types, even producing their own in 1928. Noted for its hand-forged metal bodywork, the Buffalo company had a reputation for stylish fire engines and produced some fine looking sedan-cab pumpers in the 1930s and 1940s. Factory output increased during World War II with up to 170 fire engines of

TYPE III PUMPER	
Year	1930
Engine	6-cylinder petrol
Power	70bhp
Transmission	4-speed manual
Features	Redesigned body

various types being delivered. This was possible due to Buffalo's streamlined production facility which included two parallel lines – an innovation in fire engine production. Buffalo built their last fire engine in 1948 and from then on concentrated on manufacturing fire extinguishers.

■ ABOVE *The straight bodyline of pre-war Buffalo fire engines is evident in this preserved 1940 Buffalo Pathfinder pumper used by Winters Fire Department, California.*

■ BELOW *The deliveries of the midship-mounted pump of this restored 1931 Buffalo pumper protrude from beneath the front seats. The crew's uniforms and helmets await the call to action.*

OTHER MAKES

■ BAI
Founded in 1991, BAI Antincendi
International of Bagnolo Mella, Italy, has
produced a range of firefighting and rescue
vehicles based upon a number of
commercial chassis such as Scania, Volvo
and Mercedes. Constructed for municipal,
airport, industrial and rural fire brigades,
BAI fire engines include water tenders,
foam tenders and aerial ladder platforms.

■ BELSIZE
A number of fire engines built during the
early years of motorized fire engines used
the chassis of the Belsize Motor Company
of Manchester, England. These solidly
constructed vehicles were capable of
carrying 15m/50ft wooden wheeled escape
ladders and had rear-mounted pumps. As
early as 1912, the Belsize chassis was
being used in conjunction with 18m/60ft
wooden turntable ladders, some of which
were operated using compressed carbon
dioxide gas. By the early 1940s only a few
Belsize fire engines remained.

■ BINZ
The Binz Coachworks company was formed
by Michael Binz in 1936, in Lorch,
Germany. The modern-day Binz vehicle
list includes fire service rescue and
specialized fire engines, which are built
both at Lorch and the company's second
plant at Ilmenau.

Binz have a customer base spread
across five continents. They utilize various
short to medium-wheelbase commercial
chassis for their smaller fire service units,
such as mobile command and control, and
communication units. These include the
Volkswagen T4 and LT, and the Mercedes
Benz Sprinter series.

For the medium-size market, Binz uses
commercial 7.5-tonne chassis, such as the
Mercedes-Benz Atego or MAN, to produce

a mobile control unit or respiratory/
radiation protection tender with plenty of
working space that is capable of being
either air conditioned or heated, according
to the season, at major and/or protracted
operational incidents.

One of the largest of the Binz range of
specialized fire engines is a tractor-drawn
trailer, part of which incorporates a push-
out extension when set up on site. This
provides a 20sq m/22sq yd internal area
from which strategy for major accidents
and other serious incidents can be co-
ordinated. The overall internal space of
this trailer includes telephone exchange
and switchboard, suitable space for mobile
telephones and emergency service radio
equipment, and a conferencing area. Binz
also manufactures a range of demountable
fire service units containing rescue and
medical equipment for use at major
accidents and emergencies.

■ BMC
The British Motor Corporation (BMC) was
formed by the merger of the Austin and
Morris motor companies in 1952. The new
company produced a number of chassis
types suitable for fire engine use. These
included the LD 30cwt, which was used for
vehicles like canteen vans and high
expansion foam units, the 5-ton FG model,
used as emergency tenders, through to the
heavyweight 16-ton BMC Boxer. One of
the latter went into operational use in 1970
for Staffordshire Fire Brigade, in the UK,
as a 4x2 water carrier. It was capable of
ferrying 4,500 litres/1,000 gallons of water
to the scene of a rural fire where water
resources were insufficient.

BMC became part of the Leyland Group
in 1968 and within two years the BMC
badge was no longer in use. The last
operational BMC fire engine had been
withdrawn from service by 1990.

■ ABOVE *A Boise rescue tender of
Snohomish County Fire District, Arlington
Heights, Washington, USA.*

■ BOISE MOBILE EQUIPMENT (BME)
Boise Mobile Equipment (BME) is an
Idaho-based American build-to-order
fire engine manufacturer. Its range of fire
engines includes pumpers, rescue tenders
and a number of specialist fire and rescue
vehicles for specific operational tasks.

The design of one particular BME
pumper is characterized by its dual use as
an urban or country (wildland) fire engine.
The BME pump operator's rear pump
panel has a clever interface that places the
operator away from traffic hazards yet
allows good visibility down each side of
the fire engine. Another BME feature is the
tubular-frame design, with the rescue
tenders being built of aluminium, although
galvanneal and stainless steel versions are
also available.

■ BRACO
Braco AS of Lierskogen, Norway,
manufactures a range of fire and rescue
tenders, providing a body structure and
locker design to the precise specification of
its customers, many of whom are
Scandinavian fire brigades. With a choice
of suitable commercial chassis, Braco's fire
engine body superstructures are
constructed of 100 per cent welded
aluminium to withstand the extreme
weather conditions of a northern climate.

CAMIVA

One of Europe's largest manufacturers of firefighting equipment, Camiva, was formed in 1971 by the merger of two vehicle-building concerns, Citroën-Berliet and Guinard, and has its head-quarters in the French Alps at St Alban Leysse, near Chambéry. The company produces a wide range of fire engines, including various types of water tenders for urban and rural use, and airport and industrial foam tenders. It is one of the world's leading makers of turntable ladders. Camiva's turntable ladders are used by brigades requiring a compact

high-rise vehicle for use in areas with restricted access. Camiva exports over half its fire engines to fire brigades in more than 80 countries worldwide.

■ ABOVE *This 1988 Camiva EPA 30m/100ft turntable ladder is mounted on a Dennis F127 chassis, with bodywork by John Dennis Coachbuilders.*

CARMICHAEL

Carmichael International is a British fire engine manufacturer and bodybuilder whose origins go back to the 1950s. Since then, the Carmichael works at Worcester, England, have produced a very large number of fire vehicles, including water tenders, airport foam tenders, rescue tenders, turntable ladders and hydraulic platforms, for UK and overseas fire brigades. Today, Carmichael makes the claim that it is the only UK company to produce a fully comprehensive range of firefighting vehicles. Seventy per cent of its production is exported to more than 80 countries around the world.

Over the years, Carmichael has utilized a wide range of chassis types and makes in the construction of its fire engines. These have included well established names such as AEC, Albion, Bedford, BMC, Commer, Dennis, Dodge, Ford, Land Rover and Leyland. More recently, in addition to Carmichael's own chassis, the list has grown to include IVECO, Mercedes, Scania, Timoney and Volvo.

■ LEFT *A 1970 Carmichael-bodied Land Rover 4x4.*

■ BELOW *A 1987 Dennis RS135/ Carmichael breathing apparatus tender.*

■ RIGHT *Fitted with a front-mounted winch, this unusual long-wheelbase General Motors/Carmichael rescue tender is in service with Gloucestershire Fire and Rescue Service, England.*

In 1972 Carmichael innovatively lengthened a Range Rover chassis at its factory by inserting an extra trailing axle to provide a 6x4 configuration. Powered by a 3.5-litre V8 petrol engine, this stretched Carmichael Range Rover proved especially suitable for road accident work on the UK's expanding motorway network. Over the next seven years 37 such vehicles, equipped with a front-mounted 900-litres/ 200-gallons-per-minute pump, went into service as fast-response emergency/ rescue tenders.

An example of a modern Carmichael airport crash/foam tender is the Cougar, which was built on a Timoney 8x8 chassis for delivery to British Airports Authority Fire Service, London Stansted in 1993. The 18-litre Detroit diesel engine with 825bhp gives an acceleration of 0 to 80kmh/50mph

inside 32 seconds. Carrying 12,000 litres/2,666 gallons of water and 1,500 litres/330 gallons of foam concentrate, the Cougar can project up to 4,500 litres/1,000 gallons of foam per minute from its roof-mounted monitor.

The current Carmichael International range of airport crash rescue tenders includes the 6x6 Cobra 2,000 model, which can carry up to 14,000 litres/ 3,000 gallons of water. With the largest crew cab and doors on the market, it can carry five firefighters. Carmichael has become the first UK fire engine manufacturer to use the new clean-

emission Euro 3 Caterpillar C18 4-stroke diesel engine in a number of its vehicles.

Carmichael's range of water tenders includes the lightweight LPA model, which is based on a General Motors or a Land Rover chassis and is fitted with a 1,135-litre/250-gallon water tank with a foam-making capability. Modern standard-size Carmichael water tenders have an innovative fibreglass body and tend towards Dennis, Mercedes, Scania or Volvo chassis. Carmichael also builds a number of hydraulic platforms with a working height of up to 54m/177ft.

CEDES

Cedes Electric Traction, Austrian pioneers of electric vehicles including trolleybuses, produced its first battery-electric fire engines in the early 1900s for London Fire Brigade, who were looking for an alternative propulsion method for its fire engines. The drawback with self-propelled steamers was that precious time was lost whilst sufficient steam pressure was built up to move the engine. Although the Cedes battery-electric models were ready for instant turnout they were slow moving, especially on hills, and could not travel far without having to be recharged. In addition to the ten new Cedes pumping fire engines it commissioned, London Fire Brigade converted eight of its old horse-drawn wooden Magirus

■ LEFT *Batteries weighing 2 tons were stored beneath the bonnet of this 1905 Cedes electric pump escape, used by London Fire Brigade.*

22M/75FT TURNTABLE LADDER	
Year	1908
Engine	two electric motors
Power	36hp
Transmission	direct chain driven
Features	two tons of batteries

30m/100ft-turntable ladders to work on the Cedes chassis. With the rapid development of the petrol engine, however, the move into electric traction was short-lived and by 1922 all London Fire Brigade's electric fire engines had been rebuilt on a motor chassis or withdrawn from service. Cedes itself went into liquidation in 1916.

CENTRAL STATES FIRE APPARATUS

In the 1970s, Lyons, South Dakota, USA, suffered a series of fires that prompted the start of the business known today as Central States Fire Apparatus. Harold and Helen Boer set up their welding and vehicle refurbishment enterprise in the mid-1970s, while Harold was the Chief of Lyons Volunteer Fire Department.

■ RIGHT *A 1989 Mack MC/Central States pumper.*

By the end of the decade, Central States was building fire engines, averaging 50 a year for various fire departments in America's mid west. The

■ LEFT *In service with Tuckwilla Fire Department, Washington, this Central States rescue/special operations unit is based on a 1996 International S4900.*

company grew rapidly and was soon employing 140 workers at its 8,900sq m/96,000sq ft manufacturing base. In the 1990s, it was one of several companies that came together to form Rosenbauer America, with the aim of providing a base for exporting American fire engine manufacturing expertise and design.

Central States' first custom-built pumper, constructed in 1983 on a Ford chassis for South Dakota Volunteer Fire Department, is still in general use. The current Central States range of fire engines includes pumpers, specialist tankers, aerials and rescue tenders.

CHEVROLET

The American Chevrolet chassis was used for a number of fire engines during the 1920s and 1930s. Chevrolet trucks were built in the UK for several years from 1928 onwards, and a number of these were used as non-pumping fire engines before the Bedford company produced its own Chevrolet version for the British market. After World War II, Chevrolet pumpers could be found in service in several brigades in Europe as well as the United States. A typical American 1970s Chevrolet pumper would use the 3.7m/145in COE chassis with a V8 petrol engine and was fitted with a 3,400-litre/750-gallon water pump and a 1,600-litre/350-gallon water tank.

■ RIGHT *This Chevrolet/FMC mini pumper 4x4 has a mid-mounted pump and is powered by a 235bhp V8 petrol engine.*

■ ABOVE *This preserved 1937 Chevrolet pumper once served with Kittanning Fire Company, Pennsylvania, USA.*

■ RIGHT *This Chubb Pathfinder 6x6 foam tender is in service at Hong Kong Airport.*

CHUBB

Chubb Fire Security Ltd, the British fire protection company, was prominent in the early 1970s in designing a new generation of airport firefighting and rescue vehicles in response to the growing size of wide-bodied passenger aircraft such as the Boeing 747. The Chubb Pathfinder 6x6 airport crash tender, introduced in 1974, had a number of new features, such as a central driving position and a huge roof-mounted foam monitor capable of projecting 61,300 litres/13,500 gallons of foam per minute on to a burning aircraft or fuel fire. The Pathfinder was

built on a Reynolds Boughton chassis and powered by a V6 Detroit diesel producing 635bhp.

During the 1970s Chubb built a number of high-output foam tenders for petrochemical fire brigades, but the company is particularly noted for the pump water tender it launched in 1975. The Pacesetter was the result of design collaboration between Merseyside Fire

Brigade and a subsidiary of Loughborough University. Built on a Boughton high-performance chassis, it incorporated innovative fibreglass and alloy bodywork that included a six-man crew cab with easy-access power-operated doors and a low floor line. A 238bhp rear-mounted Detroit Diesel engine drove a 4-speed automatic gear-box capable of reaching 64kmh/40mph within an impressive 18 seconds. The 4,500-litres/1,000-gallons-per-minute fire pump was mounted on, and access-ible from, the front of the fire engine.

■ LEFT *A 1991 Chubb National Foam 16m/53ft Telesquirt tender.*

■ BELOW *A Chubb Protector 6x6 foam tender with a high-output foam monitor.*

CITROËN

The chassis of this Paris-based truck and car manufacturer were used for many years to produce a range of fire engines that included water tenders, light pumps, forest-fire tenders, foam tenders and turntable ladders.

At the lightweight end of the range, the 1970 3m/117in-wheelbase, 350-

chassis, with a 95bhp, 2.2-litre petrol engine, was available in a 4x4 option. Heavier Citroën models provided the base for the 30m/100ft Metz turntable ladders used by many French fire brigades, including the Paris brigade.

In the late 1960s Citroën took a major holding in the Berliet Automobiles

Company, which itself had become a successful builder of fire engines destined for French brigades through its commercial and municipal truck division. In 1971 Berliet-Citroën combined with Guinard to form the new Camiva company, which produced a considerable number of fire engines.

COMMER

Commer chassis were built at the company's Dunstable plant in the UK, and in the years following World War II gained considerable popularity among fire brigades around the world as well as in the UK. One of the earliest post-war models was the QX chassis, which had a 6-cylinder under-floor petrol engine with 109bhp and was fitted with a 2,270-litre/500-gallon water pump. With a 3.6m/141in-wheelbase, this chassis was used extensively for rural fire brigade water tenders to provide a modestly priced, relatively compact, lightweight (6.5 tons) fire engine. From 1954 Commer utilized the new 3-cylinder 2-stroke Tillings Stevens 4.75-litre diesel engine and continued to provide water tender chassis into the 1970s. The 3-ton KC40 model, introduced in 1961, provided the chassis for a number of lightweight

■ LEFT *Formerly used by London Fire Brigade, this 1913 Commer YC pump is still in working order.*

■ BELOW *A 1950 Commer FC water tender exemplifies the evolving style of post-war British fire engines.*

■ LEFT *A c.1950 Commer pump escape of Carmarthenshire Fire Brigade, Wales.*

■ BELOW LEFT *A c.1960 Commer pump escape carries a 13m/45ft wheeled ladder.*

■ BELOW RIGHT *A 1976 Commer Hi Line G-1211 water tender used by Harwell Fire Brigade, England.*

COMMER FC	
Year	1950
Engine	6-cylinder petrol
Power	109 bhp
Transmission	4-speed manual
Features	under-floor engine

specialist fire engines. From 1960 the heavier Commer 86A 7-ton chassis was used for a number of 30m/100ft Magirus turntable ladders, with bodywork by David Haydon. In 1963 a Commer VAC was utilized for a Simon SS65 hydraulic platform for Monmouthshire Fire Brigade in Wales, the first of its type to go into operational service in the UK.

Commer ceased production of chassis suitable for fire engine use in 1975.

CROWN

■ LEFT *This 1976 Crown pumper is owned by Los Angeles County Fire Department, in California.*

Although Crown Firecoach, based in Los Angeles, California, USA, began building buses in 1904, the first Crown fire engine appeared only in 1951. Since then the company's fire vehicles have seen extensive service in American fire departments, and several have been exported to customers as far away as the Gulf States. From its early days, Crown focused on producing a single standard open cab, 3m/117in-wheelbase pumper that could be customized to any specification required. Crown also manufactured aerial ladders, both rigid and articulated 30m/100ft versions, drawn by tractor units. However, from 1980 the company concentrated on providing pumpers with various specialist applications, such as a Snorkel platform, if required. Noted for their chassis strength and longevity, one particular Crown safety feature is the suspension system that allows for the vehicle ride height to be varied according to its overall load.

■ LEFT *This 1967 Crown pumper went into service at Second Street Station, Watsonville Fire Department, in California.*

■ BELOW *A 1981 Crown pumper of Marysville Fire Department, Washington, USA, is fitted with a 6,800 litres/1,500 gallons per minute midships pump and a 2,270-litre/500-gallon water tank.*

CUSTOM FIRE

■ BELOW *This 1992 Custom Fire 5,700-litres/1,250-gallons-per-minute pumper is built on a Ford L8000 chassis.*

Custom Fire began building its first fire engines at its base in Osceola, Wisconsin, USA, in the late 1970s and has grown steadily ever since. Today it occupies 4,200sq m/45,000sq ft of factory floor space and delivers up to 36 new fire engines per year to many fire departments throughout the United States.

The range of fire engines produced includes mini and elaborate customized pumpers, heavy rescue tenders and command units. Custom Fire fire engines are unusual in that they feature a bolted body construction method

instead of the more usual welding. This type of assembly ensures easier accident reparability, as well as allowing for vehicle modification at a later date should it be required. Recently, the company shipped nine fire engine body kits to South Africa for assembly locally.

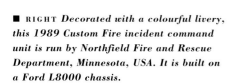

■ RIGHT *Decorated with a colourful livery, this 1989 Custom Fire incident command unit is run by Northfield Fire and Rescue Department, Minnesota, USA. It is built on a Ford L8000 chassis.*

OTHER MAKES

■ CRASH RESCUE

Formed in 1967, Crash Rescue Equipment Service, Inc, started life maintaining aircraft rescue and firefighting equipment (ARFF), and continues to undertake this work from its headquarters base in Dallas, Texas, USA.

However, in 1978, Crash Rescue started to refurbish various types of ARFF for customers across the United States and in the 1990s came the company's Snozzle equipment designed for firefighting and rescue operations. In an aviation fire engine application, the Snozzle is mounted on an elevating extendable boom. Apart from allowing the firefighting nozzle to be placed through small openings in aircraft, such as windows and doors, the Snozzle can also carry an infrared camera.

The Snozzle is also available for mid-ships mounting on pumpers, and is particularly effective for getting a rapid firefighting attack under way in a building while other larger trucks are being deployed. The Snozzle is controlled by an operator joystick.

Fire Wagons, a division within Crash Rescue, manufactures a range of specially designed functional trailers. These include carriers for firefighting foam and equipment for dealing with hazardous materials and decontamination, triage stations for attendance at major accident sites, and mobile operational command and control centres.

■ CRIMSON FIRE

Created in early 2003, Crimson Fire is a very new company name in the American fire engine industry. It is owned by Spartan Motors, Inc, and its headquarters are at Brandon, South Dakota. The company's origins actually go back to the 1990s, when Spartan Motors acquired three separate fire engine manufacturing concerns with a view to entering the fire engine market. Crimson Fire resulted from the amalgamation of two of these companies – Quality and Luverne.

Crimson Fire offers a range of fire engine types including pumpers, heavy and mini-rescue units, rapid intervention vehicles, and water tankers with a capacity up to 15,900 litres/3,500 gallons.

Aerial ladders and platforms built by Crimson Fire come both in rear and mid-mounted options. One particularly innovative product is the new E series pumper constructed of 100 per cent stainless steel.

■ CSI EMERGENCY APPARATUS

The CSI Fire & Truck company was originally formed in 1989 to provide vehicles and service facilities for the emergency services in Michigan, USA. By 1995, sales volume had increased to the point where the company moved into their own 1,300sq m/14,000sq ft manufacturing facility at Grayling, Michigan. At the same time the company name was changed to CSI Emergency Apparatus. Since the move, both production and staff levels have been doubled.

CSI Emergency Apparatus manufactures and customizes a range of fire department water tankers, pumpers and other specialist emergency vehicles.

DAF

A large number of the fire engines in use in the Netherlands after the early 1960s were built on a chassis produced by DAF, the Eindhoven-based truck manufacturer. When DAF acquired the British Leyland commercial truck company in 1987 the DAF name started to appear in fire brigades all over Europe. Since then, a number of DAF vehicles have also been built for UK use. These include water carriers (using the 16/17 and 20/210 chassis), breathing apparatus tenders (DAF Freighter), prime movers for demountable units (DAF 60), and emergency tenders on the DAF T45 as well as the

PRIME MOVER	
Year	1995
Engine	6-cylinder diesel
Power	210bhp
Transmission	manual
Features	demountable pod carrier

■ ABOVE *Designed for petrochemical use, this DAF FF1600/Rosenbauer foam tender carries a high-discharge foam monitor.*

■ ABOVE *A Dutch fire service DAF 1100 water tender typical of a number in service throughout Europe.*

1718 model used by the emergency support unit of Gloucestershire Fire & Rescue Service. This fire engine, following a trend in the equipment specification of other similar tenders, was equipped with a rear-mounted Hiab hydraulic crane for non-fire rescue work. One brigade in Lancashire, UK, commissioned over 70 DAF 60 model water tenders over a period of almost ten years. The same brigade also ran a 30m/100ft DL30 Metz turntable ladder on a DAF 1900 chassis.

■ BELOW *A 1951 Ford F Series/Darley pumper working in Pennsylvania.*

DARLEY

Based at Melrose Park, Illinois, USA, W S Darley & Co has been manufacturing fire engine water pumps since the early twentieth century. Today it combines contemporary technology with a long track record of engineering excellence. In addition to its fire pump range, Darley have built complete fire engines on various commercial chassis, such as Ford, International, Chevrolet and Duplex, for operational service in the USA and abroad. The Darley fire engine range includes custom-built pumpers, water tankers, rescue tenders, and airport foam tenders.

DENNIS

Dennis first started manufacturing motorcars and tricycles in 1895 and produced its first fire engine in 1908 for Bradford Fire Brigade, Yorkshire, England. This was followed by an order from London Fire Brigade and from then on Dennis grew from its factory at Guildford, Surrey, to become the predominant British manufacturer for half a century or more.

By the early 1930s Dennis was supplying more than 100 pumping fire engines per year to brigades throughout the UK and overseas. The very popular pump-carrying 1934 model Big Four escape, a reliable and classic fire engine of its time, went into service as far away as Hong Kong Fire Brigade. In 1937 the 250th Dennis fire engine was delivered to the London Brigade, whose pumps were still of an open-air design.

After World War II Dennis introduced the F series, with coachbuilt wooden bodies and powered either by the Dennis 3.8-litre petrol engine with

■ LEFT *The Dennis Big Four was very successful during the 1930s. This well-polished 1936 version has been lovingly preserved.*

F101 PUMP/PUMP ESCAPE	
Year	1956
Engine	8-cylinder diesel
Power	170bhp
Transmission	5-speed manual
Features	Rolls-Royce 12-litre engine

■ ABOVE *The narrow-bodied F8 was designed for rural firefighting. The vehicle's 2m/6½ft width enabled it to speedily negotiate narrow country lanes. This fine example saw long service in Devon County Fire Service, England.*

70bhp or the Rolls-Royce B80, 8-cylinder petrol engine. The F-series continued to be built into the 1970s with versions for city brigades (the 1956 F101 with a 170bhp, 12.2-litre

■ LEFT *Powered by a 150bhp 5.7-litre Rolls-Royce petrol engine, the Dennis F7 set the post-World War II standard for years to come. This 1949 London Fire Brigade pump escape was just one example of the several hundred F7s that served in British fire brigades for some 20 years.*

Rolls-Royce diesel engine) through to the best-selling narrow F8, with a width of 2m/6½ft, designed specifically for rural firefighters.

By the 1960s, when Dennis claimed to have fire engines operating in 46 countries, more petrol-engine options were being offered to increase on-road performance of the F and the newer 2.1m/7ft-wide D series. These included the Rolls-Royce 195bhp version or the Jaguar 4.2-litre. Front disc brakes on Dennis fire engines also became an option for the first time in 1962.

In 1976 the R series was introduced; it incorporated a fibreglass cab on an air-braked chassis. It was available with the Perkins V8.640 diesel engine, which gave it an impressive all-round performance. In 1979 the R series was phased out in favour of the new RS model, along with the SS tilt-cab version. These two models had a new all-steel safety cab capable of accommodating a six-man crew with breathing sets inside the crew cab area. Over 1,750 of these very successful

■ ABOVE *Now in preservation, this unusual Dennis F107 formerly served as a breakdown lorry for London Fire Brigade from 1964 until 1977. It was based at the brigade's Lambeth headquarters.*

■ RIGHT *Humberside Fire Brigade, England, operate this 1984 Dennis F133/Carmichael/Magirus 30m/100ft turntable ladder.*

■ ABOVE *This preserved 1957 Dennis F21 38m/125ft Metz turntable ladder formerly served Rochdale Fire Brigade, England.*

Dennis models were sold, mostly as pumps. However, in 1983 Dennis, then owned by the Hestair Group, took the decision to concentrate its fire engine production on chassis/cab manufacture, leaving the bodybuilding to various specialist companies.

In 1991 Dennis launched a new fire engine chassis/cab called the Rapier. This represented a complete break from the previous generation of Dennis fire vehicles, with a welded tubular space frame replacing the conventional chassis frame. The new concept gave a low overall frame height and allowed for the fitting of independent front suspension with disc brakes. The rear axle featured coil spring suspension and utilized

4.95cm/19½in wheels instead of the earlier 5.58cm/22in version. Other standard features included anti-lock brakes and traction control. All this meant that the Rapier was exceptionally stable due to its low centre of gravity. A Cummins C-series 8.3-litre engine with 250bhp driven through an Allison 5-speed automatic gearbox gave the Rapier a road performance unmatched by most of its rivals, with a 120kmh/75mph top speed allied to impressive cornering and braking ability.

In 1994, Dennis introduced the Sabre chassis/cab, which included a number of further technical refinements. The Sabre was powered by a Cummins 295bhp Euro 3, 6-cylinder diesel engine. The latest Dennis model, the Dagger, is designed for use as a compact water tender, yet provides a payload and performance almost equal to that of a conventional full-size water tender.

DODGE

■ LEFT *This 1979 Dodge/HCB Angus 1313 series water tender served in Gwent Fire Brigade, Wales.*

■ LEFT *Whatcom County Fire District, Washington, ran this 1977 Dodge/ LaFrance Custom 400 4x4, 1,135 litres/250 gallons per minute light pumper.*

Having begun fire engine manufacture during World War II, Dodge produced vehicles in the USA and UK. The American versions were from the parent Chrysler Motor Corporation range and included the 4x4, ¾-ton, T214 model, which had originally been used as a battlefield ambulance but converted readily into a pumper for use by country fire departments. From the late 1940s, the ⅝-ton, D500 chassis with a 5.2-litre, 6-cylinder petrol engine appeared in a number of pumper applications.

The later Power Wagon 4x4 chassis, an American Dodge that provided rugged cross-country performance, saw much operational service as a rural firefighting unit. Its chassis was also utilized for medium-sized airfield rapid intervention vehicles. With a Chrysler V8 230bhp petrol engine with automatic transmission, the Power Wagon was capable of an impressive 80kmh/50mph in 15 seconds and its monitor could deliver 12,000 litres/2,666 gallons of foam per minute.

In the UK, a large number of Dodge fire engines were built as pumps, aerial ladders and other special types, with bodies by a variety of bodybuilders. Early pumps were based on their 3-ton lorry chassis. In the 1970s, the K and G range provided a wider load span, from the K850 and the later 100 series G13 5-ton range for water tenders, through to the K2213, which was rated at 22 tons, and suitable for turntable ladders and hydraulic platform use. The K850 had a Perkins V8 diesel engine and a tilt cab, whilst the G13 had a more powerful Perkins V8.540 diesel engine allied to a 6-speed

■ RIGHT *This preserved 1949 Dodge/ American pumper is fitted with a 2,270-litre/500-gallon tank and the same capacity per minute midships pump.*

gearbox. The Dodge water tender's 1,800-litre/400-gallon water tank fed a Godiva pump.

From the early 1970s a large number of turntable ladders, including Magirus and Metz models, and Simon hydraulic platforms were built on Dodge heavy chassis, in particular the G1613 and G16C range. The company also built a number of specials, including foam tenders, emergency tenders and control units. In addition, several bodybuilders used the American Power Wagon Dodge chassis for their medium-sized airfield crash and foam tenders, whilst the 1979 Dodge 50 series was used by industrial

fire brigades for light pumping/first strike fire engines. By the late 1970s, a number of Dodge G series chassis had started to appear as prime movers for various demountable equipment pods.

Dodge was acquired by Renault in the early 1980s and the old badge was soon replaced by that of the new logo. One of the last British Renault/Dodge engines went into service in 1995 with Avon Fire Brigade. As a custom-built road/rail support unit for emergency calls to the 5km/3-mile River Severn rail tunnel, its chassis incorporates a set of rail wheels to run on railway lines in the event of a railway emergency incident.

DUPLEX

The long-established American firm of Duplex is well known, particularly for the specialist combination fire engines it built for US fire departments. These R-300 series vehicles combine an aerial ladder with a pumper in order to perform a dual operational role. They are powered by a Detroit Diesel BV71 2-stroke engine with Allison automatic transmission. The midships-mounted aerial ladder reaches up to 26m/85ft. A 2,270-litre/500-gallon water tank and a 5,700-litre/1,250-gallon, midships-mounted pump are also carried making this fire engine self-contained.

■ TOP *Finished in a golden yellow livery, this 1973 Duplex/Van Pelt pumper served with Alameda County Fire Department, Dublin, California.*

■ ABOVE RIGHT *Farmington Fire Co, Delaware, USA, run this gleaming 1994 Simon/Duplex 6x4 water tanker.*

■ RIGHT *The striking white livery makes this bodyline-styled, 1995 Simon/Duplex 6x4 rear-mount, 31m/102ft aerial ladder platform highly visible. It serves with Rohoboth Beach Fire Department, Dover, Delaware.*

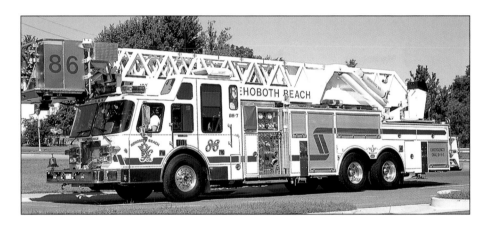

OTHER MAKES

■ **DAVID HAYDON**
David Haydon Ltd, a specialist fire engine bodybuilding and engineering company based in the West Midlands, England, built a number of Magirus 30m/100ft hydraulically-powered turntable ladders under licence during the late 1950s. These ladders, together with the bodywork supplied by the company, were built on to various chassis, such as Bedford, Leyland and AEC. David Haydon also built the bodywork of a number of customized pumping and specialist fire engines, such as the Leyland Firemaster.

■ **DELAHAYE**
Like a number of other early car manufacturers, the French company Delahaye, which was founded in 1898 and is based at Tours and Paris, soon turned its skills to fire engine design. By 1907, when mechanized firefighting methods were first being developed, Delahaye had produced a pumping fire engine that, in addition to carrying hose reels and various hose connections and fittings, was capable of transporting 15 firemen to a fire.

Over subsequent years Delahaye fire engines were supplied to fire brigades throughout France and Europe. In 1926, a number of Delahaye pumping engines were built to the specific requirements of the Sapeurs Pompiers of Paris, the regimental fire brigade that safeguarded the nation's capital, setting the future standard for European fire engines. These rear-mounted pumps had a 1,800 litres/400 gallons per minute capacity, and provided detachable hose reels to provide firemen with maximum operational flexibility.

Delahaye merged with Hotchkiss in 1954 and within two years the Delahaye large vehicle operations came to an end.

EMERGENCY ONE (UK) LTD

■ BELOW *A 1995 Mercedes 1124F/ Emergency One (UK) water tender.*

■ BENEATH *White-liveried fire engines are rare in the UK. This 2002 Scania G94 230/ Emergency One (UK) water tender serves with Grampian Fire Brigade, Scotland.*

Having delivered its first water tender to Strathclyde Fire Brigade in 1991, Emergency One (UK) Ltd is a relatively new fire engine producer. Over the past decade, the company, which is based in Strathclyde, Scotland, has continued its impressive development and won orders for a considerable number of water tenders and other specialist firefighting and rescue tenders. These have come from every one of the eight Scottish fire brigades, as well as a number of English brigades. Emergency One (UK)'s fire engines are usually based on Mercedes Benz, Scania or Volvo chassis.

■ ABOVE *This 2002 Volvo FL6/Emergency One (UK) water tender of Hampshire Fire & Rescue Service, England, carries a 13.7m/45ft alloy extension ladder.*

■ RIGHT *In 2002 Bedfordshire and Luton Fire & Rescue Service, England, received this Scania/Emergency One water tender.*

WATER TENDER	
Year	2002
Engine	6-cylinder diesel
Power	260bhp
Transmission	automatic
Features	range of rescue equipment

EMERGENCY ONE (E-ONE)

Having started life in 1974 at its Ocala headquarters in Florida, USA, Emergency One (known throughout the American fire service as E-One) is one of the newer American fire engine manufacturers. In a relatively short time it has rapidly built up an enviable reputation for its products, and delivered thousands of fire engines of all types to fire brigades in over 80 countries.

From the start the company promoted a prefabricated modular style of bodybuilding that enabled its fire engines to be attractively priced and swiftly manufactured; in many cases delivery from time of order is as little as 90 days. The bodies are mounted on a variety of suitable chassis types, including Ford, Freightliner and General Motors.

Early Emergency One models included the Protector pumper range, which featured a midships-mounted pump, and had a water tank capacity of up to 3,400 litres/750 gallons. Later Protector versions came with a tilt-cab facility. Another popular model was the

Midi-Pumper, on a General Motors 4x4 chassis, designed for rural firefighting. With a 3,400 litres/750 gallons per minute midships-mounted pump and a 2,270-litre/500-gallon water tank, the vehicle provided a

powerful firefighting attack that could be taken across most rural terrain. In 1980 Emergency One built a number of Snorkel telescopic booms on to a combination fire engine that was capable of operating as a pumper with

■ **LEFT** *A 1994 KW/Emergency One 6x4 Rescue tender in service with Claymont Fire Department, Delaware, stands at the roadside.*

■ **BELOW LEFT** *Syncrude, Alta, Canada, operate this 1997 Emergency One HPR 8x8 with a 15m/50ft Snozzle. This specialist fire engine has a 7,360-litre/1,620-gallon tank and a 12,700-litres/ 2,800-gallons-per-minute pump capacity.*

■ RIGHT *Built in 2000, this Emergency One Cyclone II 6x4 rear-mount 30m/100ft aerial ladder serves the City of Seattle Fire Department, Washington.*

an aerial firefighting arm. At the same time the company produced a number of successful compact 29m/95ft aerial ladders mounted on a 2-axle chassis. These innovative aerials were much shorter than the big and somewhat unwieldy rear-steer tiller fire engines then in use by a number of American urban fire departments.

Before long, E-One had developed its high-rise firefighting and rescue models to include the Strato Spear range. Embracing 33m/110ft aerial ladders, platforms and telescopic boom fire engines, these were at the time claimed to be among the highest aerials in the USA. The four-section ladders of the Strato Spear aerial ladder were constructed of welded aluminium, which, coupled to an underslung jacking system, made a stable working base.

E-One has continued to develop the use of extruded rust-resistant aluminium in its construction methods, claiming that it is possible to mount the resultant lighter bodies on less costly chassis options. This in turn allows fire vehicles to carry more payload, with a less negative impact on braking systems, drivelines and axles. Virtually every type of firefighting and rescue vehicle is now built at the company's five manufacturing plants.

Today E-One is the largest division of the Federal Signal Corporation, which in

■ RIGHT *In service with Delta Fire Rescue, British Columbia, Canada, this 1997 Emergency One Cyclone TC/Superior 6x4 tanker carries 11,300 litres/2,500 gallons of water, an 8,000-litres/1,750-gallons-per-minute pump and 108 litres/24 gallons of foam compound.*

■ OPPOSITE *This 1985 Emergency One Hurricane 6x4 rear-mount 33m/110ft aerial ladder now serves with Victoria Fire Department, British Columbia, Canada.*

1995 also acquired Bronto Skylift, the world-leading Finnish aerial platform manufacturer. Another significant acquisition in 1998 was the Saulsbury Fire Rescue Company. This undoubtedly added to the overall size and strength of Emergency One's products.

Emergency One fire engines can be found in many guises right across the USA and around the world. Current models include the following: the Cyclone II Industrial pumper with remote-control roof-mounted dual foam monitors with flow rates up to 18,000 litres/4,000 gallons per minute; the Titan HPR foam tender range which comes in 4x4, 6x6 and 8x8 options; aerial ladders and platforms ranging from the Typhoon HP 75 23m/75ft and the CR 30m/100ft to the HP 32m/105ft.

■ BELOW *The first all-Emergency One-built aerial fire engine was this 6x4 33m/110ft rear-mount aerial ladder, which entered service in 1984 with Washington State's Mercer Island Fire Department.*

ERF

Originally founded in 1933 by Edwin Richard Foden, ERF Ltd of Sandbach, UK, was an established manufacturer of heavy goods vehicles when in 1966 it launched two new chassis aimed at the fire brigade market. The lighter of the two, the F-series 84 RS model, was designed for water tender use, whilst the heavier F-series 84 PF was designated for mounting turntable ladders and hydraulic platforms. These ERFs were powered by either a Perkins V8 510 or 540 diesel engine with automatic transmission. Standard UK water tender specification included the choice of a 2,270-litres/500-gallons or a 4,500-litres/1,000-gallons-per-minute pump.

The interest in the new ERFs, both in the UK and abroad, was such that in 1972 a subsidiary section called the ERF Fire Division was established on a new factory site at Winsford, Cheshire, to build and assemble the ERF chassis and associated fire engineering elements. In 1977 a new company,

■ ABOVE *A preserved 1971 ERF F-series water tender attends a rally.*

entitled Cheshire Fire Engineering, took over the ERF fire engine business, although this remained wholly owned by ERF. Many ERF water tenders and hydraulic platforms built in the late 1960s and 1970s were bodied by Hampshire Car Bodies-Angus.

The ERF hydraulic platforms, some of which were powered by Rolls-Royce 8-cylinder B81 engines, used the Simon SS range, giving working heights of 20–28.3m/65–93ft. A smaller number of ERF 30m/100ft turntable ladders were manufactured during this period using Metz and Magirus ladder sections.

ERF ceased manufacturing fire engines in 1982 and by the early 1990s

few ERFs remained in operational service. However, ERF re-emerged in 1996 when several new fire engines, all on the ERF heavy duty EC 8 series chassis, went into service in the UK. These vehicles included foam tenders for Cheshire Fire Service, aerial ladder platforms (by Simon) and demountable unit prime movers for West Midlands Fire Service, and foam tenders for Greater Manchester Fire Service. In addition, Wiltshire Fire Brigade commissioned an ERF EC10-chassied Italmec hydraulic platform.

EXCALIBUR

Excalibur CBK Ltd, based at Stoke-on-Trent in Staffordshire, England, is a specialist fire engine bodybuilding company. It produced its first two firefighting vehicles – a Bedford water tender and a Land Rover light pump –

VOLVO FL6 14 WATER TENDER	
Year	1996
Engine	6-cylinder diesel
Power	265bhp
Transmission	automatic
Features	carries rescue equipment

for Powys Fire Brigade, in Wales, in 1986. Since then Excalibur CBK has grown progressively to become a prominent manufacturer of a range of pumping fire engines, water tenders and emergency/rescue tenders, which it supplies to a significant number of brigades across the British fire service. Excalibur has used a number of chassis makes for its fire engines, including Renault-Dodge, Dennis, Mercedes and Volvo.

■ LEFT *New to England's Lincolnshire Fire and Rescue Service in 1996 was this Volvo FL6 14/Excalibur rescue pump.*

FAUN

Faun-Werke GmbH, based in Nuremberg, Germany, has long been associated with firefighting equipment but is particularly noted for the large airfield crash and foam tenders it built during the 1970s. These vehicles were some of the first of the new generation fire engines developed to provide fire protection for the larger aircraft then coming into service, such as the Boeing 747. The Faun LF1410/52V, produced in 1970, was a massive 8x8 crash tender powered by a 1,000hp Daimler/Benz V10 diesel engine with 4-speed automatic transmission, able to reach 100kmh/62mph in 65 seconds.

Weighing 50 tons, it was at the time one of the world's biggest fire engines. The fire engineering equipment was supplied by Metz and included an 18,000-litre/4,000-gallon water tank and a 2,000-litre/440-gallon foam tank.

■ ABOVE *This Faun/Sides 8x8 foam tender is in service at Palma Airport, Majorca, with its powerful roof-mounted foam monitor. The high ground clearance and all-wheel drive of these heavy specialist fire engines show how they are able to respond to an incident off the airport runways.*

■ BELOW *A 1999 Ferrara Fl-RK 33m/110ft 6x4 rear-mount aerial ladder.*

FERRARA

The origins of Ferrara Fire Apparatus go back to the late 1970s when Chris Ferrara, a volunteer firefighter with Central Volunteer Fire Department, together with several colleagues, began a quest to build a new tanker fire engine for their fire department. After many hours and much hard work, the new tanker was finally commissioned at a

INFERNO PUMPER	
Year	2003
Engine	6-cylinder diesel
Power	350–500hp
Transmission	automatic
Features	extensive locker space

considerable saving to the department's funds. This success led, in 1979, to Ferrara founding a firefighting equipment company which enjoyed successive growth and steady expansion, including the refurbishment of a range of American fire engines. Then in 1988 Ferrara Fire Apparatus built its first own-brand fire engine. Today, the

■ LEFT *A 1999 Ferrara pumper of Harvey Fire Department, Los Angeles, USA. This has a midships-mounted pump and roomy rear cab accommodation for a crew of six firefighters.*

company is ranked amongst the top five fire engine builders in the USA. Ferrara Fire Apparatus Incorporated now constructs a wide range of pumpers, rescue tenders and aerial platforms. Ferrara fire engines are available on the company's own custom chassis range, which includes the Interceptor, the Gladiator, the Penetrator and the heavier Intruder model used for aerial platforms.

The heavy-duty Ferrara aerial has an operating height of 33m/110ft. Ferrara fire engines are available with modular extruded aluminium or corrosion-resistant bodies. Fire pump capacities are 4,500–8,000 litres/1,000–1,750 gallons per minute, whilst variable water tank sizes of 2,270–9,000 litres/ 500–2,000 gallons are available.

Ferrara also custom-builds various types of fire engines on to other commercial chassis models, including those of International Harvester and Duplex.

■ ABOVE *A 1995 Ferrara Intruder pumper with a 4,770-litres/1,050-gallons-per-minute pump and 3,980-litre/875-gallon tank.*

■ BELOW *This Marrero Fire Department, Los Angeles, 1999 Ferrara/Inferno rescue tender has plenty of locker room.*

FIAT / OM

Based in Turin, Italy, Fiat has been manufacturing cars since 1899, but most of its chassis were produced by its commercial subsidiary, OM of Brescia. For many years OM chassis provided the base for a wide range of water tenders, airport crash tenders and foam tenders used for refineries.

The OM 150 series was used throughout Italy in the 1970s and 1980s. This 4-ton chassis boasted a 3,000-litre/660-gallon water tank and a high-pressure pump. The OM 260 series six-wheeled chassis was also used for larger foam tenders, where its 15-litre, V8 diesel engine with over 300bhp allowed significant water and foam payloads. OM chassis are also used for Italy's forest firefighting tankers, which carry 4,000 litres/880 gallons of water on the heavy-duty TLF chassis.

A number of light fire engines have also been produced using the Fiat 1,300 T2 van and the jeep-style Fiat Campagnola 4x4. Many of these vehicles carry modular units, including a 400-litre/88-gallon water tank and portable pumps, lighting units and other ancillary firefighting gear.

Today, Fiat's commercial arm is the IVECO group (Industrial Vehicle Corporation), which came into being in 1975. Under its own badge, it produces various chassis types for use by a large number of fire brigades around the world.

FIAT/OM 260	
Year	1982
Engine	V8 diesel
Power	300bhp plus
Transmission	6-speed manual
Features	6x4 heavy foam tender

■ LEFT *Belonging to Vigili Del Fuoco, this c.1950 Fiat light 4x4 is in use as a general-purpose and support firefighting vehicle, particularly for rural incidents.*

■ LEFT *This c.1985 Fiat light 4x4 fire engine owned by Del Fuoco Fire Brigade, Italy provides general back-up duties in rural areas.*

■ BELOW *A 1992 Fiat 14 long-wheelbase general-purpose utility fire engine of Kellinghusen Fire Brigade, Germany.*

FORD

By 1915 Ford Model T cars were being used by many US fire chiefs. The New York Fire Department modified a Model T for firefighting duties. Despite its short wheelbase, a number of Model Ts soon went into service across the USA, while in Britain the Ford A and BB series chassis were used for a number of compact open pumps during the 1930s.

The arrival of the Ford V8 engine in 1932 provided the type of performance that was especially suited to fire brigade use. The British government supplied the Auxiliary Fire Service with a large number of 8-cylinder V8 30hp Fordson 7V Thames series for use as wartime heavy pumping engines. But it was not until after World War II that Ford chassis saw increased use as fire engines around the world.

In the 1950s Ford medium-size chassis, such as the F5 series, were particularly popular. In the Netherlands the F5 model formed the basis of a water tender with a front-mounted 3,000-litres/660-gallons-per-minute pump feeding

■ BELOW *The fine wooden bodywork and fittings of this preserved Dutch Fire Service 1938 Ford V8 light pump are a rare sight. This fire engine towed a dry powder unit, which in pre-war days was a relatively new firefighting feature.*

■ RIGHT *A Harrow Fire Brigade, England, crew aboard this c.1938 Ford lightweight pump. At that time, provision for crew in an American-style body was unusual for a British fire brigade.*

■ BELOW *A good example of early post-war fire engine development is this c.1950 Ford 30m/100ft Magirus turntable ladder, seen here in service at the Knokke-Heist Fire Brigade station, in Belgium.*

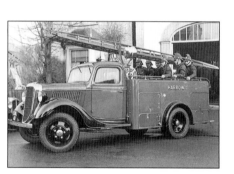

■ ABOVE *Operated by Falck Redningskorps, a private Danish fire service, this c.1980 Ford D1114/Magirus 30m/100ft-turntable ladder puts in an appearance at a German fire engine rally.*

■ BELOW RIGHT *A 5,700-litres/1,250-gallons-per-minute pump is carried by this 1985 Ford C8000/Van Pelt/FMC pumper.*

three hose reels from a 2,000-litre/440-gallon water tank. In Germany, in the mid-1950s Ford G398TA 4x4 chassis were used for water tenders.

In the 1970s American Ford light-weight pumpers included those on the short-wheelbase 4x4 Super Duty N1000 chassis and on the 4x4 F6000 series. These had a 4,500-litre/1,000-gallon water tank and a 3,400-litres/750-gallons-per-minute midships-mounted pump. Major American Ford pumpers used both the L series chassis of the 1970s and the 3.4m/135in C series. The latter came with a tilt cab, 276bhp engine and automatic transmission air brakes, a 4,500-litres/1,000-gallons-per-minute pump and a 2,270-litre/500-gallon water tank.

In the UK, during the 1950s and 1960s, the 4D Thames (3.6-litre diesel engine) and heavier Trader chassis (5.4-litre diesel) were popular for water tender or emergency/rescue tender use. In 1965 Ford launched the improved D series 4 to 10-ton chassis with a 6-litre engine. Over the next 10 years,

■ BELOW *A 1976 Ford C617/InterContinental tractor unit functions as a fire safety classroom.*

large numbers of water tenders were built on the Ford D1014 3.4m/134in chassis for county fire brigades, together with emergency and foam tenders, hose layers, prime movers and other specials using the heavier D1317 and 1617 series Ford with the Perkins V8 540 engine.

A number of Ford A series 3.5–5.5-ton chassis with a 2.4-litre diesel engine

also went into service in the UK, mostly as compact rescue tenders. For some years, the ubiquitous Ford Transit, particularly the 130 and 160 series, has been extensively modified for fire service use across Europe, usually as lightweight or first response fire tenders.

In 1986 the commercial vehicles division of Ford was acquired by IVECO.

FORT GARRY INDUSTRIES (FGI)

The Canadian fire engine manufacturer Fort Garry Industries (FGI) began life in 1919 as an automotive repairer and distributor. In the early 1950s, the company built its first fire engine for a small-town fire department in Manitoba. However, it was not until 1979 that FGI took the decision to manufacture fire engines as a core part of its overall business activities.

FGI built its first modern fire engines, two pumpers for their local Winnipeg fire department, in 1986. These were built on a Kovatch chassis, believed to be the first in Canada. The following year it produced a number of pumpers for use in Winnipeg, based on a Spartan chassis. It built its first aerial ladder in 1989 and since then has used virtually every variety of North American aerial ladder for its high-rise fire engines.

In 1992, FGI entered into an agreement with Pierce to become the exclusive Canadian distributor of Pierce

■ ABOVE *This 1996 Freightliner FL70/Fort Garry Industries rescue tender was built for service in the MOA Nickel Company, Cuba.*

RESCUE TENDER	
Year	1996
Engine	6-cylinder diesel
Power	350hp
Transmission	automatic
Features	front-mounted winch

■ BELOW *A brand new 2003 Freightliner F61/KW T300 pumper is about to be delivered to Kapuskasing, Ontario, Canada.*

■ LEFT *This 1996 Fort Garry/Pierce Lance pumper was delivered to Cuba. It can pump 4,770 litres/1,050 gallons of water a minute.*

fire chassis and aerial ladders. When this agreement expired in late 1997, FGI agreed a two-year arrangement with American LaFrance to build pumpers using the Eagle chassis.

Over the past 30 years and more, FGI has delivered over 1,500 fire engines to fire departments across Canada, and to several in the United States. It has also exported its fire vehicles to over 15 countries, including China, Cuba, Pakistan and the United Arab Emirates.

In 2000, FGI moved into a larger modern plant in Winnipeg. It now produces a very wide range of fire engines, including pumpers (both mini and regular), rescue units and aerial ladders. The 27 different types of vehicle are available in more than 2,500 different options.

FRASER

Founded in 1953, the Fraser Engineering Group of Lower Hutt, New Zealand, incorporates a specialist fire vehicle section, which manufactures a range of fire engines for fire brigades of both New Zealand and Australia. The vehicles include heavy pumpers for urban use, foam tenders, industrial pumpers and airport crash tenders.

Altogether, Fraser has built some 200 different fire engines, including 100 units delivered over the last decade. Recently, the company delivered a batch of heavy pumper units, all based on the Scania 94D-260 chassis, to the Metropolitan Fire Service of South Australia.

HEAVY PUMPER	
Year	2002
Engine	diesel
Power	260bhp
Transmission	manual
Features	high-output water pump

■ ABOVE *With Lowes Industries no longer in business, South Australia turned to another New Zealand manufacturer, Fraser Fire and Rescue Limited, to augment its pumper fleet. This Scania 94D-260 2002 example features a Waterous pump.*

FREIGHTLINER

■ BELOW *New Westminster Fire Department, British Columbia, Canada, operate this 2001 Freightliner/SVI rescue tender. The Department's motto is carried on the vehicle's sides.*

Founded in 1939 and based in Portland, Oregon, Freightliner has become one of America's major heavy-duty truck manufacturers. When a fire department requires a bonnet-hood type configuration for a fire vehicle, several American fire engine manufacturers, including Emergency One, choose the heavy-duty Freightliner chassis. Freightliners are also used when an all-wheel drive is required. Freightliner tractor units are utilized to draw various heavy articulated fire applications, such as trailer-borne command and control units.

FL80 PUMPER	
Year	1996
Engine	6-cylinder diesel
Power	350hp
Transmission	automatic
Features	4,540 l/1,000 gpm pump

■ LEFT *A 1999 Freightliner/Hackney rescue and air tender sports an eye-catching livery.*

■ BELOW *This 1996 Freightliner/ 4-Guys tanker has a 13,600-litre/ 3,000-gallon tank.*

GENERAL MOTORS

Since the 1950s the General Motors Corporation of America (GMC) has manufactured a number of special chassis that have been used by fire brigades as pumpers, rapid intervention vehicles and emergency tenders. By the 1960s, a number of GMC fire engines could be found in the Netherlands, including those providing a base for Magirus turntable ladders.

In America the GMC 7,500 series with a V6 engine was a popular choice for compact pumpers. Front-mounted

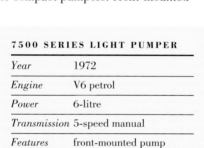

7500 SERIES LIGHT PUMPER	
Year	1972
Engine	V6 petrol
Power	6-litre
Transmission	5-speed manual
Features	front-mounted pump

■ BELOW *A long-wheelbase 1997 General Motors T8500/Hub pumper of Sasamat Fire Department, Belcarra, British Columbia.*

pumps were available on this GMC chassis configuration giving outputs up to 5,700 litres/1,250 gallons per minute. A 4,500-litre/1,000-gallon water tank could be fitted to this model. From 1985 the later K3500 chassis with a Chevrolet engine was also popular with a number of UK bodybuilders, including Saxon Sanbec, American Vehicles and Angloco, for emergency/rescue tender use. Several of these GMC emergency/rescue tenders have been built with a stretched wheelbase to improve their overall equipment carrying capacity.

GENERAL SAFETY

■ BELOW *Grand Forks Fire Department, North Dakota, USA, run this 1987 Spartan/General Safety pumper.*

■ BOTTOM LEFT *This 1975 Ford C8000/General Safety pumper carries a 3,400-litre/750-gallon water tank and pumps 4,500 litres/1,000 gallons a minute.*

Correctly known as General Safety Equipment, this company was founded in 1929 in Wyoming, Minnesota, by the grandfather of the current president, Kevin Kirvida. The continuing family involvement over the years has helped General Safety establish a proud tradition of quality and innovation.

The company's achievements were marked in 1950, when its production work for military bases received the US Army/Navy E Award, the highest recognition given to civilian companies.

Today, General Safety manufactures a range of finely crafted pumpers, aerials, airport crash tenders and industrial fire engines.

Together with Rosenbauer International, Central States and RK Aerials, General Safety is a partner in Rosenbauer America. This joint enterprise was formed in the 1990s to use the partner companies' combined expertise in technology, design, manufacturing and other resources to provide an American base for the export of US-designed fire engines.

■ LEFT *A spacious rear crew cab is a feature of this 1993 Kenworth/General Safety heavy pumper.*

■ BELOW *A 1992 Freightliner/General Safety pumper carries a 20m/65ft Snorkel boom.*

PUMPER	
Year	1992
Engine	6-cylinder diesel
Power	350hp
Transmission	automatic
Features	19m/65ft snorkel boom

GLOSTER SARO

Gloster Saro, a member of the British aircraft manufacturer Hawker Siddeley Group, built a number of specialist airport foam and crash tenders, in particular for the Royal Air Force. Earlier models used the Thornycroft 6x6 Nubian chassis with a Rolls-Royce B81 engine, together with 4,500-litre/ 1,000-gallon water tank and 225-litre/ 50-gallon foam concentrate tank.

In 1979 Gloster Saro introduced the Javelin 6x6 model, which was capable of a foam discharge rate from the large roof-mounted monitor of 45,500 litres/ 10,000 gallons per minute. The lighter Meteor 4x4 model also became available at around the same time. Other Gloster Saro airfield foam and crash tenders designed for military use were based on the Scammell low-line chassis.

■ RIGHT *The central driving position is a feature of this 6x4 Simon/Gloster Saro Protector heavy foam tender.*

JAVELIN FOAM TENDER	
Year	1979
Engine	V16 diesel
Power	600bhp
Transmission	automatic
Features	45,400lpm/10,000gpm output

GRUMMAN/HOWE/OREN

This American fire engine manufacturer, which has its headquarters at Roanoke, Virginia, is also well known for the fighter planes it has built for the US Navy for many years. The direct involvement of Grumman Allied Industries, Inc, in fire engines, dates from 1968 when it acquired the Howe-Oren Company, a long-established joint manufacturer of American fire engines.

The Howe element of this company had built horse-drawn pumps as far back as the 1880s and delivered its first motorized pumper in 1908 before going on to construct hundreds more over the following years. In 1965, Howe bought the Oren Company, which at the time was a much smaller manufacturer of

■ ABOVE *In service with Whatcom County Fire District, Evershon, Washington, this 1984 Chevrolet Kodiak Grumman pumper incorporates a 4,500-litres/1,000-gallons-per-minute pump and a 4,500-litre/1000-gallon water tank.*

■ RIGHT
*Jamestown Fire
Department, North
Dakota, runs this
1983 6x4
Grumman
29m/95ft aerial
ladder. It is fitted
with a 6,800
litres/1,500 gallons
per minute fire
pump.*

traditional pumpers for American fire departments. Grumman soon brought a new and modern styling to the Howe-Oren range of fire engines, at the same time introducing a new series of its own custom-built pumpers.

These vehicles went under the name of the Firecat, Minicat and Wildcat series, depending, among other things, on their pumping and water tank

capacity. The Grumman Firecat was available on various commercial chassis, such as Ford, International Harvester and GMC. The aluminium-bodied Minicat series came on a Ford or Chevrolet chassis and was designed primarily for a fast, all-terrain cross-country ability, where its 1,350-litres/ 300-gallons-per-minute pump could be used to good advantage.

■ RIGHT *Tacoma
Fire Department,
Washington, run
this 1989 Spartan
Gladiator/
Grumman pumper.*

■ BELOW *This
white-liveried 1988
6x4 Grumman
tanker is in service
with Rohoboth
Beach, Delaware.*

OTHER MAKES

■ GFT INTERNATIONAL
GFT International GmbH manufactures a prolific number of fire engines at its factory in Munich, Germany, and delivered an impressive 2,000 fire engines over a recent ten-year period. The wide range of firefighting and rescue vehicles, which includes water tenders, turntable ladders, aerial platforms, airfield crash tenders and hose layers is based on various commercial chassis, especially Mercedes and MAN.

■ GRÄF & STIFT
In addition to trucks, Gräf & Stift of Vienna, Austria, produced a range of fire engines. After World War II, heavier Gräf & Stift fire engines such as turntable ladders were mounted on the 120KN chassis fitted with a 120bhp diesel engine. This chassis was robust enough to accommodate a 30m/100ft-turntable ladder. The company's range of lightweight fire tenders was expanded in the late 1950s by their merger with the Vienna-based truck manufacturer OAF. Many OAF light fire tenders were built on the A90, 1.5-ton, 4x4 chassis, which carried a portable 750-litres/165-gallons-per-minute pump.

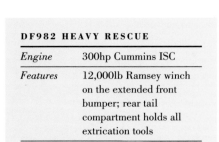

HACKNEY

Soon after it was founded in 1946, the American company Hackney began specializing in truck bodies for the delivery of consumer beverages. The introduction of the all-aluminium side-load, roll-up door body occurred in the 1960s and demand for this developing technology led Hackney to open a second, more modern manufacturing plant in 1972 at Independence, Kansas. Today, the company is the world's largest producer of side-loader, overhead door truck bodies and trailers.

Hackney built its first purpose-built fire engine in 1984 for the fire department in Salem, Oregon. This was termed an emergency support vehicle

DF982 HEAVY RESCUE	
Engine	300hp Cummins ISC
Features	12,000lb Ramsey winch on the extended front bumper; rear tail compartment holds all extrication tools

and soon a number of other American fire departments had convinced Hackney of the growing need for a new generation of rescue and support tenders to carry the ever increasing amount of specialist equipment used in fire and rescue operations.

Today, the dedicated fire engine division known as Hackney ESV is a

leader in the design and build of rescue fire engines and emergency support units. These include heavy, medium and light rescue units, rescue/pumpers, mobile air units (for replenishing and servicing breathing sets at the scene of major incidents), hazardous material trailers, and incident command units. Hackney have recently developed a

prototype rescue pumper fitted with a water pump mounted on a Freightliner FL70 with four-door cab. The company claims that the prototype has more than twice the equipment storage capacity of any of its competitors with an equal wheelbase. This rescue tender has a 2,270-litres/500-gallons-per-minute pump, 1,135-litre/250-gallon water tank.

■ BOTTOM
A HME/Hackney heavy rescue unit delivered new in 2002 to Luling Fire Department, Louisiana.

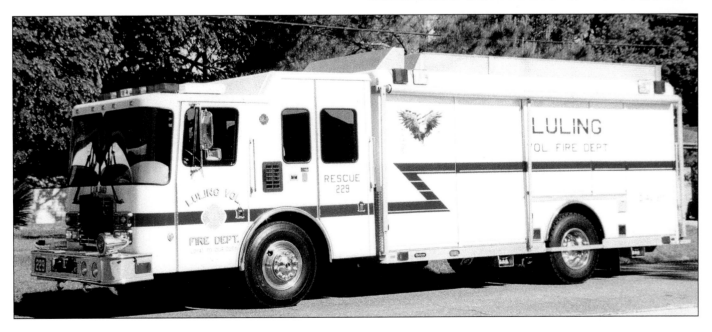

HAHN

Hahn Motors Incorporated had their manufacturing base in Hamburg, Pennsylvania, USA. Founded in 1923, the company built a significant number of durable and reliable fire engines, including pumpers, tractor-drawn, rear-mounted aerial ladders, and rescue/salvage tenders for fire departments across the USA. Unusually for a medium-sized manufacturer, Hahn built their own custom fire engine chassis, which for some time was also used by other smaller fire engine manufacturers. Hahn also utilized a number of commercial chassis, such as those of fire engine manufacturer International, for its vehicles, depending on a fire department's particular technical specification.

After World War II, Hahn's forward control fire engines were designed with an identifiable rounded frontal shape to their crew cabs. During the 1970s a typical Hahn tractor-drawn aerial ladder unit was powered by a General Motors

CUSTOM	
Year	1973
Engine	V8 diesel
Power	350hp
Transmission	automatic
Features	tractor for aerial ladders

V8 Detroit diesel delivering 350bhp through an Allison automatic transmission. Such an aerial fire engine would be fitted with a Grove 30m/100ft centre-mounted ladder, which, due to its considerable length was provided with a

■ BELOW *Lime Rock Fire District, Rhode Island, operates this powerful 1988 Hahn HCP12 pumper.*

■ RIGHT *Blades Fire Company, Delaware, owns this 1970 International/ Hahn pumper.*

■ BELOW RIGHT *This 1984 Hahn rescue and salvage tender is operated by Milford Fire Company, Delaware.*

■ BOTTOM *A 1930 Hahn pumper of the Brandywine Hundred Fire Company, Bellefonte, Delaware.*

rear-steer tiller cab. A 908-litres/200-gallons-per-minute inbuilt pump was fitted to provide an independent basic firefighting attack. In the 1980s, the Hahn HCP 12 pumper was a popular choice with many East Coast fire departments and a number of these were built with pumping capacities up to 6,810 litres/1,500 gallons per minute.

Hahn ceased production in 1990, although a number of the company's fire vehicles, including some that have been refurbished, remain in active service with American fire departments.

HME

More correctly known as Hendrickson
Mobile Equipment, Inc, HME is the
largest independent builder of custom
fire engine chassis in North America.
Founded in 1913, it is widely recognized
for a tradition of technological
innovation. From its manufacturing
headquarters at Wyoming, Michigan,
HME builds fire engines not just for
American fire departments but also for
diverse customers around the world. The
company utilizes the latest computer
technology for its customized fire engine
design in order to accommodate every
conceivable special feature that a fire
department may require.

HME fire engines display the
company's Maltese cross logo as a
symbolic badge of those who risk their
lives for others.

The company's custom fire engine
range includes the 1871 series of
pumper chassis, aerial ladders and
platforms. The numbering of the 1871
chassis range is a deliberate recognition
of the year of the Great Fire of Chicago
as well as the company's own historical
origins close to the city.

■ ABOVE *This
1984 Hendrickson/
Van Pelt pumper
can deliver 4,500
litres/1,000 gallons
per minute.*

■ LEFT *A 1979
Hendrickson/Van
Pelt pumper of
Anderson Fire
Department,
California.*

The 1871 custom pumper chassis has
a number of options, including the
1871-SLe, which is the basis for the
HME/Ahrens-Fox name, together with
the 1871-P, 1871-SFO Silver Fox and
1871-P2 models. The stainless steel
body provides for side or centre hose
stowage, 2,270-litre/500-gallon water
tanks and huge compartment space.

A full line of HME's aerial ladders
and platforms comes in working heights
of 18–31.7m/60–104ft, with a
2,270-litre/500-gallon water tank and
4,540-litres/1,000-gallons-per-minute
pumping capacity. Among a host of high
performance and safety features is a
radio control system that permits remote
operation of the aerial and its nozzle.

■ LEFT *The fire
engine fleet of
Kent Fire
Department,
Washington,
includes this 1996
6x4 HME/Smeal
32m/105ft rear-
mount aerial
ladder.*

■ RIGHT *This International/HME/Boise Mobile Equipment heavy rescue tender was delivered in 2000 to Barrington Fire Department, Arlington Heights.*

■ BELOW LEFT *This unusual white and blue-liveried 1974 Hendrickson/Clark pumper is seen standing on the forecourt of the Fire Department's firehouse at Sparks, Nevada. Fitted with a 6,800-litres/ 1,500-gallons-per-minute pump and a 3,400-litre/750-gallon water tank, this fire engine also carried 250 litres/55 gallons of foam concentrate.*

HINO

■ ABOVE *A 1996 HME 1871/Central States pumper in Washoe County, Nevada.*

A number of this Tokyo-based car and truck manufacturer's chassis are suitable for fire brigade use. The first Japanese firefighting and rescue hydraulic platform, used by Tokyo Fire Brigade, was built on an open-cab Hino chassis. In the 1970s the Hino 6x2 twin-steer heavy COE chassis was used to mount a 32.6m/107ft turntable ladder powered by a Hino DK10 200bhp diesel engine. It had air brakes, a water tank and an integral fire pump as well as a searchlight and a spray system at its top to protect the firefighter from radiated heat.

Hino also build a range of water tenders on the Ranger chassis, as used by Tokyo Fire Brigade. They have a midships-mounted 2,200 litres/484 gallons per minute water pump and a 2,500-litre/550-gallon water tank. Other Hino chassis, such as the FH22 range, are in service outside Japan as water

■ ABOVE *A Hino FH22 OKD 4x4 water tender in operational service with the Cyprus Fire Service stands at the ready.*

■ RIGHT *A Hino 6x4/Morita Super Gyro 30m/100ft aerial ladder platform serves in Japan's Miyazaki Fire Department.*

tenders for both city and rural firefighting use.

Some of the most recent Hino chassis, particularly the low-profile 6x4 configurations, are utilized for aerial ladder platforms. These fire engines include the Morita 30m/100ft aerial ladder platform, fitted with an elevator facility and a midships-mounted pump.

HONDA

Many fire brigades with serious access problems in parts of their territory make use of the range of lightweight and mini-pumping fire engines produced by Tokyo-based car manufacturer Honda.

MINI PUMP	
Year	1988
Engine	twin-cylinder petrol
Power	250cc
Transmission	manual
Features	4x4

■ LEFT *Together with eight others, this Honda Sunward mini 4x4 is used by the Hong Kong Fire Service on offshore islands, where access to property can be difficult.*

Hong Kong Fire Service, for example, runs nine Honda Sunward mini-pumps (among the world's smallest fire engines), to negotiate narrow thoroughfares and lanes on the offshore islands.

The Honda mini-pump is crewed by a single firefighter and comes in two versions, one equipped with a portable pump and hose to serve as a firefighting unit, the other carrying breathing sets.

HOWE

For almost 80 years, the Howe Fire Apparatus Co of Anderson, Indiana was a name to be reckoned with in fire apparatus construction. Founded in 1872 by J C Howe, the company waited more than 30 years before it built its first pumper. Within ten years productivity had increased dramatically with a US army order for 100 fire trucks to be built on Ford T chassis. Howe also utilized chassis built by Chevrolet, International, Diamond, Oshkosh, Dodge, and Duplex among others.

The company headquarters burnt down in the late 1930s but the incident did not stop productivity and the corporation continued to go from strength to strength. In 1965 Howe acquired Coast Fire Apparatus, a rival manufacturer, but was itself bought out by the Grumman Corporation in 1976. Fire engines continued to be manufactured under the Howe logo for several years, but in 1983 productivity ceased and the Howe name disappeared from the market.

■ ABOVE: *A 1971 Ford L900/Howe pumper, Lake Samish Fire Department, WA.*

■ BELOW *This 6x4 Howe/LTI 26m/85ft rear-mount aerial ladder dates from 1976.*

HUB

Founded in 1959, in Matsqui, British Columbia, Canada, HUB built its first fire engine, an F-series Ford pumper, in the same year. The company grew steadily and by the 1960s was constructing a range of fire engines on various commercial chassis, including International, Ford and GMC, for fire departments across Canada. By 1979, HUB was also using Mack chassis for its pumper range.

In 1986, HUB entered the aerial fire engine market through an agreement with British manufacturer Simon Snorkel. At that time Simon hydraulic platforms were rare in Canada. Several HUB/Simon aerials were manufactured over the next few years, including a 31.4m/103ft Simon model mounted on a Mack series R chassis destined for North Vancouver Fire Department.

■ ABOVE *A 1986 6x4 Peterbilt/HUB/Simon 23.5m/77ft hydraulic platform used by Colwood Fire Department, BC, Canada.*

■ LEFT *Port Coquitlam Fire Department, British Columbia, run this 1988 Ford CF8000/HUB heavy rescue unit.*

From 1988 to 1991, HUB was the Emergency-One dealer in Canada, and in 1998, a further partnership with LaFrance was struck. This collaboration saw the first of a range of HUB fire engines being built on the Eagle chassis for Canadian fire departments. The company continues to expand its output.

PUMPER	
Year	1996
Engine	6-cylinder diesel
Power	275bhp
Transmission	automatic
Features	high-output pump

■ ABOVE LEFT *A 1996 Freightliner FL80/HUB pumper.*

■ LEFT *An early example of a North American Snorkel was this 1972 23m/75ft 6x4 Inc–Co/HUB.*

OTHER MAKES

■ **HANOMAG-HENSCHEL**
When the two long-established German truck manufacturers Hanomag and Henschel merged in 1968, each company had already built hundreds of water tenders and compact light fire engines. Many of these vehicles had 4x4 drive, including the 1967 Hanomag F45 series. The 1967 Henschel HS100 series 4x4 diesel engine water tender had a 1,500-litres/330-gallons-per-minute pump and a 2,000-litre/440-gallon water tank.

■ **HAYES**
Daniel Hayes, an American engineer, built the first high-reach wooden aerial ladder mounted on a turntable base in 1868 for San Francisco Fire Department. Requiring the combined efforts of six firemen, his new horse-drawn ladder could be wound up to 26m/85ft. The Hayes aerial heralded a revolution in high-rise firefighting techniques. Before then the maximum height of firefighting ladders had been around 15m/50ft, but these earlier slim-width ladders were often unstable. Hayes disposed of the rights of his ladder design in 1882 to the LaFrance Steam Engine Company, which in 1903 became part of the much larger American LaFrance organization.

INTERNATIONAL

INTERNATIONAL

■ BELOW *Leipsic Delaware Fire Company took delivery of this brand new International heavy pumper in 2000.*

With several manufacturing bases in the USA, International has produced a number of commercial truck chassis that have been used for fire engine construction, including light and standard pumpers and rescue tender applications. For many years, the International chassis included a bonneted-cab layout, and in 1970 a forward-control version was available.

In the 1970s a Ward LaFrance-bodied International T73–250-IHC1800-10 pumper used a 4.3m/169in International Loadstar 1800 chassis powered by a V8 engine and fitted with a 1,135-litres/250-gallons-per-minute pump and a 4,500-litre/1,000-gallon water tank. A number of International-chassied Darley water tenders were built for the newly nationalized New Zealand Fire Service in 1976, and Australian-built International chassis were used for water tenders and turntable ladders by both the South Australian Fire Service and New South Wales Fire Brigade.

■ BELOW *A 1980 International 6x4 tractor provides the pulling power for this Houston Fire Company, Delaware, water tanker.*

■ RIGHT *This military firefighting and rescue tender utilizes a heavy-duty International 6x6 chassis.*

■ BELOW *A 1969 International Fleetstar/Superior (USA) of Shoshone County Fire District, Pinehurst, Idaho.*

■ BELOW *Typical of modern Australian urban fire engines, this International 1800/ACCO water tender belongs to New South Wales Fire Brigade. It is shown here standing at the ready outside Kent Street Fire Station in Sydney.*

ISUZU

The Japanese motor manufacturer Isuzu has produced various types of fire engines for many years. Among the first of the modern generation was the TXG20 of the 1960s, which was used for many water tenders. This open-cab vehicle had a 2,250-litre/500-gallon midships-mounted pump, a 3,000-litre/660-gallon water tank and water monitor.

Isuzu chassis are also used for mounting Morita turntable ladders, such as the 40m/130ft model. In the early 1970s Isuzu was also using its low-profile YZ20 tandem-axle chassis, powered by a 10.1-litre, 6-cylinder engine with 195bhp, as a base for the Morita turntable ladders, including the 40m/130ft version. This heavy

Isuzu/Morita turntable ladder weighed just over 20 tons and incorporated a fire pump to provide firefighting water.

■ RIGHT *Northern Territory Fire Service runs this 4x4 rural fire tender. The robust vehicle has a high ground clearance and open-backed equipment storage.*

■ ABOVE *Japanese-built Isuzu chassis are increasingly used for Australian fire engines, such as this heavy rescue tender.*

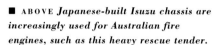

IVECO

IVECO (Industrial Vehicles Corporation), the commercial wing of Fiat of Italy, became involved with the manufacture of fire engines soon after it acquired the German Magirus-Deutz in 1975. This commercial truck concern was also a long-standing builder of firefighting vehicles and before long the famous Magirus fire engines were bearing the IVECO name.

Magirus has also long been associated with turntable ladders and the IVECO 120, 140, 192 and 256 chassis have all been widely used as a base for Magirus turntable ladders, which continue to appear under the Magirus name.

Kent Fire Brigade, in England, was one of the first British brigades to order the new 30m/100ft Magirus DLK23 turntable ladder mounted on the new low profile IVECO 120 Magirus. Three were delivered for immediate operational use in 1997.

■ LEFT *A 2000 4x4 Iveco Magirus compact hydraulic platform/pump.*

■ BOTTOM LEFT *An Iveco Euro-Mover/Magirus 30m/98ft turntable ladder with fitted rescue cage await delivery in 2000.*

■ BOTTOM RIGHT *An Iveco/DAF 19.463 4x4 heavy rescue tender.*

JOHN DENNIS COACHBUILDERS

When in 1984 the British, Hestair-owned Dennis company ceased building complete fire engines to concentrate on producing specialist chassis, John Dennis (grandson of one of the original founders of Dennis Brothers in 1895) decided to set up his own bodybuilding company. Thus in 1986 the infant John Dennis Coachbuilders bodied its first Dennis fire engine chassis, and within two years the company had developed to utilize its first non-Dennis chassis. By 1990 John Dennis's business had grown to the extent that the company had to move into a larger purpose-built factory in Guildford, Surrey, England.

Over the past 20 years John Dennis has built up an enviable reputation for quality. In 1995, the company achieved UK market leadership for the first time, with nearly half of Britain's fire brigades as customers. Today it builds a range of fire engines for the wider European market, including light water tenders, rescue and emergency tenders, animal-rescue vehicles, multi-purpose refinery vehicles, command and control units, hose layers and operational support units. In addition to traditional water tenders based on Dennis, MAN, Mercedes Benz, Scania and Volvo chassis, John Dennis also builds specialist fire engines on other chassis such as Steyr Pinzgauer, Mercedes Unimog and Land Rover.

DENNIS SABRE	
Year	1994
Engine	6-cylinder diesel
Power	295bhp
Transmission	5-speed automatic
Features	Cummins Euro 3 engine

■ TOP, ABOVE AND LEFT *The locker stowage of a typical 1994 John Dennis Coachbuilders/ Dennis Sabre TSD233 water tender was impeccably designed. This vehicle was built for Wiltshire Fire Service, England.*

OTHER MAKES

■ JAY-FONG

The Jay-Fong factory in Manchuria, China, has been building large numbers of standard fire engines for use throughout China since the mid-1950s. Based on the Jay-Fong CA-10 bonneted chassis, its standard fire engine came in either a water tender form or a water tanker version. Jay-Fong water tenders have front or midships-mounted water pumps and a six-man crew cab. Jay-Fong also produces a Chinese jeep-style 4x4, used extensively as light pumps for firefighting in remote rural areas.

■ J C MOORE INDUSTRIES

J C Moore Industries is one of the oldest manufacturers and refurbishers of fire engines in the eastern part of the USA. Based at Fredonia, Pennsylvania, the company has a model range that includes pumpers, both urban and mini, tanker pumpers, brush units and other tenders.

Recent J C Moore fire engine deliveries have included a pumper tanker on an International chassis, with stainless steel body, 11,350-litre/2,500-gallon tank, and 4,540-litres/1,000-gallons-per-minute pump. Another J C Moore tanker/pumper with a similar body, tank and pumping capacity was mounted on a Mack Granite chassis, although this vehicle had a front-mounted pump. A further new delivery, a straight pumper used a GMC chassis with 4,540-litre/1,000-gallon tank and 5,700-litres/1,250-gallons-per-minute pump.

■ JEEP

The American Jeep chassis is in operational use with a number of fire brigades on both sides of the Atlantic, especially as a fast-response rescue tender. The Jeep 320/40 model has a 3-litre V8

petrol engine, and in the tandem-axle configuration can quickly carry a considerable amount of heavy rescue equipment to the scene of an emergency.

■ BELOW *A 1968 6x6 Jeep fire and rescue tender on duty in Delaware.*

■ BOTTOM *This Jeep 4x4 light brush pumper serves with Linfield Fire Company, Pennsylvania.*

KENWORTH

Both forward-control and snub-nosed Kenworth chassis are used by a number of American fire engine bodybuilders, including Maxim and Crown for pumpers, rescue tenders, water tankers and custom-built tractors used for drawing 30m/100ft aerial ladders. The Kenworth Maxim S Type pumper has a powerful midships-mounted pump with a maximum output of 7,570 litres/1,665 gallons per minute. Kenworth 6x4 chassis are popular as the base for water tankers. The Kenworth manufacturing base is in Seattle, Washington, USA.

T300 6x4 TANKER	
Year	2002
Engine	6-cylinder diesel
Power	350 hp
Transmission	automatic
Features	13,500l/3,000-gallon tank

■ RIGHT *This handsome 6x4 Kenworth/ Darley 13,620-litre/3,000-gallon tanker was new in 2002 to Big Lake Fire Department, Skagit County, Washington.*

■ BELOW *Built in 1963, this Skagit County Kenworth 6x4 tanker has an 18,000-litre/ 4,000-gallon capacity.*

KME/KOVATCH

Founded in 1946, when John "Sonny" Kovatch Jnr acquired a modest motor repair business on his return from military duty in World War II, Kovatch Mobile Equipment (KME) is based at Nesquehoning, Pennsylvania, USA. A large part of the Kovatch organization comprises KME Fire Apparatus, which is America's largest privately owned fire engine manufacturer.

Today, KME is an industry leader in the production of custom-built special vehicles for a variety of markets across the world. The current range includes pumpers, rescue tenders, wildland vehicles, airport rescue and firefighting trucks, industrial foam tenders, water tankers and a variety of aerial ladders and firefighting platforms.

Customized chassis are constructed to the design requirements of a particular fire department in aluminium, galvannealed steel or stainless steel. Computer-controlled plasma burners and punch presses are an important part of the manufacturing operation. Fire chiefs have a choice of over 300 different configurations of crew cab.

■ BELOW *A 1998 KME mid-mount rear-steer aerial ladder.*

■ LEFT *This fine-looking 1998 KME pumper is in service with Little Creek Fire Company, Delaware.*

■ BELOW *A 1997 KME custom-built rescue tender is operated by The Citizens' Hose Company No 1, Smyrna in Delaware.*

The KME and Kovatch organization headquarters covers over 28 hectares/70 acres, with around 700 workers in 12 plants. Four other production sites are located in California, New York, Massachusetts and Virginia.

OTHER MAKES

■ KARRIER

During the 1950s and 1960s a number of emergency, rescue and salvage tenders were built for British fire brigades by various bodybuilders using the British Karrier Gamecock 2.9m/115in-wheelbase 3–4-ton chassis. These were lightweight derivatives of the Commer commercial chassis range and ultimately all Karrier lightweight vehicles were produced under the name of the parent company.

■ KAWASAKI

The Japanese company is better known for motorcycles, but Kawasaki's engineering skills led to the production of some of the world's smallest fire engines. The Kawasaki Mule, for instance, has been designed with a custom-made body to provide a basic first-aid firefighting response in areas where access for full-sized fire engines is difficult, such as in pedestrianized sectors and old urban centres. The Mule two-seater 2510 model, just 1.3m/4¼ft wide and 2.9m/9½ft long, has 4-wheel drive and carries a portable pump and hose.

■ ABOVE *The Kawasaki Mule is a two-seater first-aid firefighting vehicle for areas with restricted access.*

■ KRONENBURG

Kronenburg BV of Hedel, the Netherlands, has manufactured fire engines since the nineteenth century. In the 1950s and 1960s their water tenders, for urban and rural use, used British or American chassis, including Austin and Chevrolet.

In the late 1960s a typical Kronenburg airfield crash tender utilized a DAF V1600BB358 4x4 chassis with a 6-cylinder, 155bhp engine. It had a 2,000-litre/440-gallon water tank, a 400-litre/88-gallon foam compound tank and a roof-mounted monitor that could be operated from within the cab. But to keep up with the increasing size of passenger aircraft, Kronenburg built a large 6x6 crash/foam tender on an FWD 0-153-L6 chassis. Powered by a Waukesha V8 engine with 330bhp, this vehicle had a 6,000-litre/1,320-gallon water tank, a 1,200-litre/264-gallon foam tank and a 2,800-litres/600-gallons-per-minute pump that fed roof-mounted and ground-level monitors.

In 1996 Kronenburg supplied the British Airports Authority Fire Service with 17 6x6 airport foam/crash tenders for service at London Heathrow, Gatwick and Stansted airports.

■ KRUPP

The German truck manufacturer Krupp, based at Essen, built a significant number of fire engines both before and after World War II. These included LF16 water tenders, rescue tenders, turntable ladders using both Metz and Magirus ladder mechanisms, and a number of heavy rescue crane trucks (Kranwagens). The Krupp name eventually ceased to be associated with fire and rescue vehicles.

■ LEFT *This Kronenburg 6x6 foam/crash tender serves at Heathrow.*

■ BELOW *A preserved 1950 LF 16 Krupp water tender.*

■ BOTTOM *This 1940 Krupp heavy pump was in service with Kasterlee Fire Service, Belgium.*

LAND ROVER

In 1948 the British Rover Motor Company produced its first 4x4 Land Rover, designed primarily for agricultural and utility use. From the earliest days, a number of rural fire brigades around the world purchased Land Rovers to operate as lightweight fire engines, as these were capable of carrying a certain amount of firefighting and rescue equipment over rough terrain. Their operational versatility and functional construction have endured over the years, and hundreds of Land Rovers have seen service as light pumps for both rural and industrial plant use, as rescue and emergency tenders, and as other specialist vehicles.

The first Land Rovers came with a 1.5-litre petrol engine, and in a light fire engine form usually carried a short ladder, a hose reel, a built-in fire pump and small water tank, a hose, and various other firefighting equipment. The first models had a 2m/80in wheelbase and although they were an immediate success, considerable development took place over the following years to widen their performance and scope of work. In 1954, the wheelbase was extended by 15cm/6in, and the rear overhang and body provision was lengthened. A long-wheelbase version was also available with the option of a 1997cc/121.8cu in engine. Land Rover wheelbase options were extended again in 1956 to 2.24m/88in or 2.77m/109in. A year later, the first diesel engine Land Rover was produced. In 1958 the Series II models were introduced. They were slightly wider, had a restyled body and some other cosmetic changes.

Modern Land Rover light fire engines are based on the Defender 110 or 130 chassis. Common firefighting and rescue items include a cab roll cage, a

■ ABOVE *Carmichael added the extra trailing rear axle to this 1975 Range Rover 6x4 rescue tender.*

polypropylene water tank with inlet and fill system, a folding-knuckle crane and a powerful winch. A range of modules includes engine-driven soaker or fogging pumps, a hose reel, and a compressed air system that injects air into a water/foam mixture from an on-board compressor. For ease of handling by the crew, these modules can be removed from the vehicle using the electric lift facility.

■ ABOVE *This 1968 HCB Angus Firefly 109 light pump was one of many used at the time by UK rural fire brigades.*

■ RIGHT *A 1978 Land Rover 109 tows Hampshire Fire Brigade's fast rescue boat, England.*

The Range Rover model was first adapted for British fire brigade operational use in 1972, when in conjunction with Carmichael Ltd an extra trailing axle was added to provide a 6x4 configuration. This enabled a far greater equipment payload to be carried, including hydraulic cutting and lifting gear, heavy rescue tools and generators for tool power and lighting. These Range Rovers were among the first to carry telescopic lighting masts to illuminate the scene of night-time accidents and other emergencies. Powered by a 3.5-litre, V8 petrol engine, many of these high-performance, light fire engines saw service mostly in fast-response rescue/emergency tender guise, especially as motorway and road networks developed. Later Range Rover models are in use with a number of UK brigades as forward-control units and support vehicles for major incidents, especially in locations where access is difficult.

LEYLAND

Leyland Motors Ltd of Leyland, Lancashire, England, began building fire engines soon after the first motorized fire tender appeared in the early 1900s, supplying its first model to Dublin Fire Brigade in 1910. Before long, fire engine manufacture had become a significant part of Leyland's commercial business alongside its bus and truck division, and it introduced a 6-cylinder, 85bhp petrol engine specifically for fire engine use.

By the end of World War I Leyland, along with Dennis, another English firm, was beginning to dominate the fire brigade market in the UK and throughout the British Empire. The company's fire engines were put into service as far afield as Tasmania and China. Leyland produced several specific chassis for its water tenders and pumps, including the 1920 FE model, followed in 1935 by the FK6 (with a rear-mounted 2,270-litres/500-gallons-per-minute pump) and the FK7 with a 3.5m/138in wheelbase (with a midships-mounted pump). Some FK models were utilized as limousine-type pumps/emergency tenders.

Until the early 1930s Leyland turntable ladders were mounted on the Leyland LM chassis, but in 1935 the company entered into an agreement with the German turntable ladder manufacturer Metz to supply their ladder mechanisms on a special Leyland chassis. This highly successful 4.4m/174in TLM chassis was available with either an 8.6-litre Leyland diesel or a 6-cylinder, 115bhp petrol engine. The 45m/150ft Leyland/Metz turntable ladder delivered to Hull Fire Brigade in 1936 was at the time the tallest ladder in British fire service use. Some Leyland/Metz turntable ladders had built-in hydraulic jacks. Over 50 Leyland/Metz turntable ladders were manufactured before the outbreak of World War II, which brought this Anglo-German partnership to an abrupt end.

In 1939 London Fire Brigade ordered eleven Leyland FKT dual-purpose pumping fire engines. These pre-war Leyland pumps were powered by a 7.7-litre Leyland 96bhp petrol engine and could carry either a 15m/50ft-wooden wheeled escape ladder or a 10m/35ft extension ladder, and were

■ LEFT *In the 1960s some Leyland chassis were used in India as basic water tenders, such as this Delhi Fire Service vehicle.*

some of the first to have all-enclosed crew cabs. During the early stages of World War II, Leyland built over 50 turntable ladders to a government order for National Fire Service use.

After the war Leyland produced its stylish Comet truck chassis with a 5.6-litre diesel engine, and some open-cab water tender/escape ladder versions of this model went to India. The real Leyland fire engine innovation came in 1958, however, with the introduction of the Firemaster chassis. Using Leyland bus and coach parts and powered by an underfloor, midships-mounted 9.8-litre Leyland diesel engine with 150bhp, this chassis allowed the 4,500 litres/1,000 gallons per minute fire pump and its controls to be fitted at the front of the fire engine. Another unusual fire engine feature was the 4-speed semi-automatic transmission via a fluid flywheel and epicyclic gearbox, probably making this one of the first of the two pedal-controlled fire engines.

Two Magirus turntable ladders were built on the Firemaster chassis, but despite its technical features the Firemaster was not a commercial success and only a handful went into operational service.

In 1962 British Leyland acquired the AEC Company and 12 years later absorbed Albion. Various water tenders, emergency tenders and other special vehicles were built in the 1970s and 1980s using Leyland chassis, including the Laird, the Boxer, the Terrier and the Mastiff. British Leyland was acquired by DAF Vehicles in 1987 and since then the Leyland logo has gradually disappeared from fire engines in service.

■ RIGHT *A 1990 Leyland Freighter T45–180 water tender of Greater Manchester County Fire Service, England.*

■ LEFT *A preserved 1953 Leyland Comet water tender of Surrey Fire Brigade, England.*

■ LEFT *This 1987 4x4 Leyland/Daf 16/17 water tanker/foam carrier serves with Hampshire Fire Brigade, England.*

■ LEFT *In 1990, Lancashire Fire Brigade, England, commissioned this Leyland Swift/ Reeves Burgess coach as a control unit and canteen vehicle.*

LIQUIP

Founded 30 years ago, Liquip is an Australian company, based at Smithfield, Sydney, New South Wales. The organization specializes in chemical

■ LEFT *A Scania 94D 260 heavy pump of the Queensland Fire & Rescue Service.*

PUMPER	
Year	1996
Engine	6-cylinder diesel
Power	275bhp
Transmission	automatic
Features	high-output pump

and bulk liquid distribution vehicles. For a number of years Liquip have built various specialist rescue vehicles and fire engines for Queensland Fire Service, South Australian Metropolitan Fire Service, and several one-off rescue units for the mining industry, all with steel and alloy bodies. Liquip's range of specialist fire

rescue vehicles are available with two- or four-wheel drive, single or dual crew cabs, and water tank/body superstructure in a combination of steels or alloy. The company build a special 4x4 fire tender with 2,000-litre/440-gallon tank for use on sandy islands or other areas where only a 4x4 vehicle can operate.

LOWES

No longer in business, New Zealand-based Lowes Industries was a vehicle manufacturing company that for some years built a number of different fire engines, primarily for New Zealand and Australian fire brigades. The company utilized a number of commercial chassis, including Scania and Mitsubishi, and offered a standard design of light and heavy pumpers, as well as other fire engine types.

A typical 1990s Lowes light pump unit could be found mounted on a Mitsubishi FK160F chassis with a 1,800-litres/400-gallons-per-minute pump and a 2,000-litre/440-gallon water tank.

In 1997, Lowes delivered a rescue pumper bodied on the Scania 93M-250 chassis to the South Australian Metropolitan Fire Service. It featured

■ RIGHT *Lowes built a series of pumpers for the South Australian Metropolitan Fire Service on 3 and 4 Series Scania chassis. Darley 3,800-litres/840-gallons-per-minute pumps were standard.*

■ LEFT *This Mills Tui-built Lowes/Mitsubishi rescue pumper has the capacity to pump 1,800 litres/400 gallons per minute.*

conspicuous yellow striping, a front-mounted winch and roll-out rescue equipment trays. Two years later, the same brigade received a number of

Lowes pumpers on the uprated Scania 94DB-260 chassis. These fire engines were fitted with a Darley 3,800-litres/840-gallons-per-minute pump.

LTI

LTI (Ladder Towers Inc) are now part of the American LaFrance corporation. American LaFrance offer the complete range of models manufactured by LTI, including rear or mid-mounted models, together with tractor-drawn versions. They are available in aerial ladder/articulated boom aerial ladder/water tower and ladder platform configurations. The range includes the MV and AH aerial ladders at 22.8m/75ft, the 30.4m/100ft QS, and the tractor-drawn 33.5m/110ft model.

In addition, the LTI 52EL is a five or six-section ladder giving a working height of 52m/170ft, while the mid-mount LTI provides a maximum working height of 28.3m/93ft. The LTI 100LT is a 30.4m/100ft rear-mount platform.

These American LaFrance LTI aerial fire engines are available on a combination of American LaFrance, American LaFrance Eagle, or Freightliner 4x4 and 6x4 chassis.

The range of American LaFrance/Ladder Towers Inc aerial fire engines are nowadays built at two separate plants located at Ephrate and Lebanon, Pennsylvania, USA. These plants collectively employ 340 people.

■ ABOVE *A 2001 Spartan/LTI tractor-drawn, mid-mount rear-steer aerial ladder.*

■ BELOW *A 1977 6x4 Pemfab/LTI/Hamerly rear-mount aerial ladder.*

LUVERNE

The Leicher brothers acquired the Luverne Wagon Works, of Luverne, Minnesota, USA, in 1896. After the company produced its first car in 1903, it followed up with a number of motorized funeral hearses, and then its first commercial truck. In 1912 the company built the first Luverne fire engine and three years later, its first pumper. Luverne then continued steadily to develop its range of pumpers and other fire vehicles, including 75 fire engines under the Nott name, for small town fire departments.

In 1985, Luverne Fire Apparatus was purchased by Luverne Truck Equipment. This company produced bumpers, grill guards and mirrors for every manufactured truck and van in the United States. Soon after, there followed a move to a new manufacturing facility in Brandon, South Dakota.

In 1997, the ownership of Luverne was acquired by Spartan Motors, Inc,

which in the early 1990s had also purchased the Quality fire apparatus company. In January 2003, Luverne and Quality were amalgamated to form a new

■ ABOVE *This 1989 Autocar/Luverne pumper has a 6,800 litres/1,500 gpm pump.*

fire engine manufacturer, Crimson Fire, on the South Dakota factory site.

■ LEFT *A Spartan 6x4 chassis forms the base for this Minnesota-based 1994 Luverne pumper/tanker. It features a 9,000-litre/2,000-gallon water tank.*

MACK

Having started life as a maker of truck and bus chassis, Mack is one of the longest established American fire engine manufacturers. Originally founded in 1900 in Brooklyn, New York, the company moved several years later to its base at Allentown, Pennsylvania, where it subsequently became one of America's major truck manufacturers and one of its largest builders of complete fire engines of various types.

Mack produced its first tractor in 1909, designed specifically for towing fire equipment, and built its first pumping fire engine two years later. This was sold to the Union Fire Association of Pennsylvania and was soon followed by a motor-driven hook and ladder truck.

Many of the early twentieth-century Mack fire engines were built on the AC model 3½-ton truck chassis, which was soon to be adopted by the US army as the standard military truck. Following World War I, Mack army trucks had a deserved reputation for reliability and performance. As a result, Mack vehicles acquired the nickname 'Bulldog', so the company adopted the bulldog motif as

■ LEFT *This 1954 Mack pumper served in Georgetown Fire Department, Delaware.*

■ BELOW LEFT *Camano Island Fire and Rescue, Washington, run this 1981 6x4 Mack RS/Smiley's 13,600-litre/3,000-gallon tanker.*

■ BELOW *A 1981 Mack CF tractor unit pulls a mid-mount 30m/100ft rear-steer aerial ladder in Dover, Delaware.*

C95FD PUMPER	
Year	1965
Engine	6-cylinder diesel
Power	237bhp
Transmission	2-speed automatic
Features	5-man canopy cab

its insignia. The successful AC model remained in production for over 20 years.

A feature of Mack's early articulated aerial ladders was their length. One was so long that it required the rear axle to be steered by a rear steersman.

In 1935 Mack designed and built the first enclosed fire engine in the USA for Charlotte Fire Department of North Carolina. This Sedan model pump incorporated a 3,400-litres/750-gallons-per-minute pump. At this time Mack was also producing traditional bonneted pumps, with the Bulldog mascot standing proudly on the radiator cap. By then Mack fire engines had become well known for their snub-nosed cabs bearing a central circular emblem enclosing an 'M'.

After World War II, Mack continued to develop its range of fire engines. A typical early 1950s unit was the Model B95 pumper. With a six-man sedan-type

■ RIGHT *This 1991 Mack MC/Custom pumper, in service with Savage Fire Department, Minnesota, USA, has a 5,700-litres/1,250-gallons-per-minute pump and a 3,400-litre/750-gallon water tank.*

■ BELOW LEFT *New York Fire Department runs this 6x4 1981 Mack CF/Baker 23m/75ft Aerialscope.*

■ BELOW RIGHT *One of several New York Fire Department c.1980 Mack CF pumpers.*

crew cab, it was powered by a Thermodyne 276bhp petrol engine and had a 4,500-litre/1,000-gallon pump. The normal-control B95 lasted in the Mack range for 16 years before being superseded by the R611. This had a 4.3m/169in wheelbase, a three-man cab with a 238bhp Mack diesel engine and a 3,400-litres/750-gallons-per-minute pump. The CF model of the late 1960s went on to become one of the most popular pumps throughout the USA. One of Mack's most powerful pumping

units, and probably one of the world's largest fire engines at the time, was the Super Pumper System acquired by New York Fire Department in 1965. This articulated pumping unit had a De Laval pump driven by a 2,400hp Napier Deltic diesel engine that was capable of delivering 33,600 litres/7,400 gallons per minute. It was accompanied by three Mack satellite tenders, each one capable of acting as a hose layer for the 15cm/6in-diameter hose and to provide further massive water monitors.

By this time Mack was also producing 30m/100ft aerial ladders for several fire departments throughout the United States, including New York Fire Department. The company produced its Aerialscope in 1970. This fire engine was mounted on a 3-axle chassis with a 325hp V8 diesel engine driving through a 5-speed gearbox. With telescopic booms and ladder plus a three-man bucket, the Aerialscope had a very wide range of operational ability for rescue and firefighting purposes.

■ RIGHT *City of Abbotsford Fire Department, British Columbia, Canada, operates this 1985 Mack MC/HUB pumper. It is fitted with a 4,770-litres/1,050-gallons-per-minute pump and a 2,270-litre/500-gallon water tank.*

MAGIRUS

The German firm of Magirus had its origins in 1864 when Conrad Dietrich Magirus founded his company to build fire engines and firefighting equipment. In 1872 Magirus produced a wooden turntable ladder mounted on a horse-drawn carriage chassis. Its wooden ladder sections had to be wound up and rotated by hand, but from this basic start Magirus went on to specialize in and develop rotating turntable ladder technology to become a major international supplier. In 1932 Magirus built five 30m/100ft all-steel turntable ladders for London Fire Brigade, the first of these new ladders to have been supplied outside Germany.

In 1938 Magirus merged with the engine manufacturer Klockner Deutz and went on to produce a range of commercial truck chassis in addition to

fire engines under the Magirus-Deutz badge. After World War II Magirus-Deutz resumed supplying turntable ladders to a number of Europe's fire brigades, often using Leyland or Mercedes chassis as well as its own. In the 1950s the preferred Magirus-Deutz chassis for its 18m/60ft turntable ladder was the C125 fitted with a 125bhp diesel engine. The heavier tandem axle S7500, with

the more powerful air-cooled V8 175bhp diesel engine, provided the base for the Magirus 50m/165ft turntable ladder, probably the world's highest at the time. Many of these turntable ladders incorporated a fire pump to provide for the water needs when the turntable ladder was in use as a water tower.

Although Magirus-Deutz became part of IVECO (Industrial Vehicle Corporation) in 1975, the company has continued to produce turntable ladders under the original Magirus name. Recent developments have seen the use of detachable cages at the ladder head; the rigging of the ladder sections to allow for emergency use as a crane; and the incorporation of electronics technology in the aerial ladder operator controls system.

250D25	
Year	1965
Engine	V12 diesel
Power	250bhp
Transmission	6-speed manual
Features	KW16 crane wagon

■ ABOVE LEFT *A Magirus Deutz c.1990 GFW water rescue unit. This fire engine carries an inflatable boat and various other items of rescue equipment.*

■ LEFT *A 1997 Iveco 120–25 low profile Magirus DLK 30m/100ft turntable ladder with rescue cage.*

MAN

Chassis built by Munich-based MAN have been used in fire engine manufacture across Europe for some years. In the 1960s the Ziegler company provided the bodywork of a number of TLF 16 standardized German water tenders based on the MAN 450 HALF 4x4 chassis, and the HAL 4x2 version. These had a 1,600-litres/350-gallons-per-minute pump. In the UK, MAN chassis were being used on an increasing number of special fire service vehicle applications, including emergency tenders, prime movers and control units. In addition, a number of Metz 30m/ 100ft turntable ladders mounted on the 12–16-ton MAN 16D series chassis have gone into service. A

significant MAN fire service user is Devon Fire & Rescue Service, UK, which has commissioned 25 compact water tenders for rural use, using the MAN L2000 10.224F series chassis with bodywork and fire engineering supplied by British bodybuilder Saxon Sanbec.

■ RIGHT *This rescue tender was new to Stadt-Bottrop, Germany, in 1960.*

■ LEFT *A new 2002 MAN LE 280 B/Metz 30m/ 100ft turntable ladder with rescue cage destined for Germany.*

■ BELOW *A 1984 Mack MC/Marion pumper fitted with a 6,810-litres/1,500-gallons-per-minute pump.*

MARION BODY WORKS

Marion Body Works is a long established family-owned American manufacturer of engineered truck bodies. Founded in 1905 in Marion, Wisconsin, the present ownership and management have been in place since 1980.

The company's comprehensive range of fire engines includes pumpers, rescue pumpers that combine both functions within one emergency vehicle, rescue tenders, hazmat units, and tankers. In addition, Marion also manufactures aerial ladders in conjunction with Aerial Innovations, Inc.

Marion utilize either a commercial or customized chassis, depending on a fire department's specifications. Since 1964, Marion have been building fire engines with all-aluminium bodies. The versatility of Marion-built custom rescue pumpers is well illustrated by the unit that went into operational service with

Cooks Volunteer Fire Department of Charlotte, North Carolina, during 2002. This dual-purpose fire engine was built on a Spartan Gladiator chassis powered by a Detroit Diesel Series 60 430hp engine and Allison automatic transmission. The designers at Marion Body Works conceived an all-aluminium body with a six-firefighter

crew cab. It has a Waterous CSU 6,810 litres/1,500 gallons per minute water pump with side control panel and a 3,405-litres/750-gallons polypropylene water tank. Other features include a 1,500-watt lighting tower on the cab roof, a 15kW generator, and a 567 litres/125 gallons per minute foam system.

MAXIM

The Maxim company was founded in New England, USA, in 1914 and produced a range of pumpers and trucks for a number of years before turning its principal production and development efforts towards aerial ladders. In 1955 Maxim was acquired by the larger Seagrave company although the Maxim name continued to appear on various types of American fire engine for some time.

■ ABOVE *A 1975 Maxim SLT100 30m/100ft mid-mount aerial ladder.*

■ RIGHT **This 1930 Maxim B50 pumper is fitted with a 2,270 litres/500 gallons-a-minute pump.**

MERCEDES-BENZ

Currently the world's largest manufacturer of commercial trucks, Stuttgart-based Mercedes-Benz features prominently in the fire brigade market. Since World War II the company has developed many chassis suitable for fire engine use in Europe.

In the 1950s the Mercedes LAF311 4x4 chassis was widely used in Germany for water tenders, while many post-war 30m/100ft Metz turntable ladders used the Mercedes-Benz L315 heavy chassis. In the 1970s the LAF1113 4x4 chassis was extensively used for pump water tenders, with many German Mercedes fire engines being bodied by

■ LEFT *Somerset Fire Brigade, England, operates this Mercedes 1622/Saxon water carrier to supplement firefighting water in their largely rural area.*

■ LEFT *A rugged-looking Mercedes Unimog 4x4 equipment carrier belonging to Stadt-Bottrop Fire Brigade, Germany, features an HIAB hydraulic arm and front-mounted winch.*

ATEGO 1328	
Year	2003
Engine	6-cylinder diesel
Power	280bhp
Transmission	manual or automatic
Features	disc brakes on both axles

■ FAR LEFT *Stadt-Bottrop Fire Brigade, Germany, use this medium Mercedes as a hose-laying tender.*

■ LEFT *This 1992 Mercedes Unimog 2150 L special incident unit, in service with West Yorkshire Fire Service, England, has all-terrain cross-country capability.*

Metz. In 1972 the Austrian Rosenbauer company supplied domestic brigades with water tenders using the Mercedes heavy 6x4 2232 chassis powered by a 320bhp diesel engine for service in Austria. These incorporated a 3,200-litres/700-gallons-per-minute pump, a 500-litre/110-gallon foam tank and 9,000-litre/ 2,000-gallon water tank.

More up-to-date, wider Mercedes chassis include the Unimog 1.5-ton, 2150L, 4x4 all-terrain vehicle for forest and rural firefighting, the 917 and 920AF series as rescue tenders, the 1124AF as heavier payload emergency tenders, and the 1625, 1726 and 1827 series as the bases for many turntable ladders and aerial ladder platforms. The latest Mercedes Atego 1328 series chassis, with a 6-cylinder, 280bhp turbocharged diesel engine to European emission standards, and disc brakes on both axles, is much in use as a standard water tender.

MERRYWEATHER

For over 130 years the British firm Merryweather was one of the biggest names in fire engines. Its origins can be traced back to 1750 when Adam Nuttall started a company in London, England, building manual fire pumps. Through a series of partnerships, the company became Hadley, Simpkin and Lott in 1792, and was innovative in producing some of the first successful horse-drawn manuals. In 1807, Moses Merryweather joined the firm as an apprentice and by 1839 had complete control of the company. From this time the Merryweather name became synonymous with reliable fire engines the world over.

Merryweather produced its first steam-powered pump in 1861 for the Hodges private fire brigade in Lambeth, London. The Deluge, as it was called, was so successful that, just one year later, Hodges ordered a second, the more powerful 2-cylinder Torrent. These famous steam pumps were instrumental in promoting the excellence of Merryweather's products. At the Crystal Palace National Steam Engine Contest in 1863, Merryweather won first prize, after which the company found its order book full with customers at home and abroad, and went on to construct eleven steam pumps in 1865.

Another Merryweather landmark was the production in 1899 of its first self-

■ LEFT *A horse-drawn 1880 Merryweather manual pump has folded white pumping handles.*

■ BELOW LEFT *London Fire Brigade once owned this 1902 Merryweather Fire King.*

FIRE KING	
Year	1902
Engine	2-cylinder steam
Power	30hp
Transmission	chain-driven direct
Features	self-propelling

■ RIGHT *With the pump of this*
Merryweather Fire King already connected
to a fire hydrant, firemen set up a hose line
ready for action.

propelled steam fire engine, the Fire
King. Capable of providing a firefighting
water jet 45m/150ft high at 1,600 litres/
350 gallons per minute, it could attain a
speed of 32kmh/20mph on the flat. This
first model went to India, but before long
the Fire King was rapidly superseding
horse-drawn steamers in the large city
brigades at home. By the turn of the
century, Merryweather was also
producing a wide range of firefighting
equipment, from extinguishers to fire
escapes. One novel product was the
Quadricycle, consisting of two tandem
bicycles between which was suspended
a platform for hose and other equipment.

Merryweather was one of the first fire
engine manufacturers to utilize the
petrol engine. In 1903 it supplied a
combination fire escape carrier and
chemical fire engine to Tottenham Fire
Brigade in north London. Another
breakthrough came one year later when
Merryweather produced another petrol-
driven fire engine for a brigade in
Finchley, also in north London. In this
model, engine power was also used to
drive a built-in water pump. The

Finchley fire engine was the precursor
of its type, which was soon to be found
throughout the world. At this time
Merryweather also experimented with a
number of battery-electric fire engines,
although these needed to carry up to two
tons of batteries. With the rapid
development of the petrol engine for fire
brigade use, interest in electric power
soon diminished.

By 1908 Merryweather was taking a
serious interest in turntable ladders. In
this year it completed a 20m/65ft turntable ladder and innovatively used the
vehicle's engine to power the extension
and rotation of the wooden ladder
sections. The company continued to
develop its turntable ladder technology
and by the 1930s was incorporating
all-steel ladder sections, either on a

Merryweather chassis using a Meadows
or Dorman petrol engine, or on other
suitable commercial chassis. The
company's reciprocating water pumps
were by then world famous, and it also
pioneered the use of foam systems on its
pumping fire engines.

Merryweather built a large number of
turntable ladders for service during
World War II. After the war it continued
to focus attention on turntable ladder
production, where hydraulic power
replaced mechanical power for all ladder
movements from the late 1950s. The
company also provided bodywork and fire
engineering on a range of fire engines for
various fire brigades. Merryweather
delivered its last turntable ladders in the
early 1970s, after which its long-standing
name faded from the scene.

■ ABOVE *A number of Merryweather*
pump escapes were built on an AEC
Mercury chassis for the Hong Kong Fire
Service in 1961.

■ LEFT *This AEC Mercury/Merryweather*
30m/100ft turntable ladder was delivered
to London Fire Brigade in 1965.

METZ

With its origins going as far back as 1840, the German company Metz has long been associated with the manufacture of firefighting equipment, but is best known for its turntable ladders. Mounted on a variety of suitable commercial chassis, Metz ladders have served for 70 years in the fire brigades of Europe and America. In 1933 Coventry Fire Brigade, in England, took delivery of one of the first Metz all-steel ladders. By 1935 Metz turntable ladders were being offered in 26m, 27m and 30m/85ft, 90ft and 100ft variants. These four-section all-steel ladders were mechanically raised, extended and rotated, although some 1935 models had a hydraulic jacking system. In 1935 Metz entered into an agreement with the British manufacturer Leyland to supply ladders on a Leyland chassis. These vehicles, usually with the 30m/100ft four-section variant, were sold in quantity to brigades in the UK and across the British Commonwealth. In 1936 an unusual 45m/150ft five-section Leyland/Metz turntable ladder was supplied to Kingston-upon-Hull Fire Brigade; at the time it was the tallest ladder in the British fire service, and probably in the world.

Metz re-emerged after World War II to continue developing its turntable-ladder technology, particularly with the addition of a rescue cage at the head of the ladder. With a load capacity of three

■ LEFT *This c.1950 Mercedes/ Metz is typical of post-WW II German light pumping fire engine design.*

■ LEFT *A c.1990 4x4 Unimog/Metz TroLF 750 dry-powder unit of the German Fire Service.*

■ BELOW *A preserved 1954 Dennis F17/Metz 30m/100ft turntable ladder.*

persons or 270kg/595lb, this incorporates a set of controls allowing the firefighter in the rescue cage to control all the ladder movements. When not in use the cage is carried on top of the ladder. In recent years Metz have also introduced a computerized safety system that allows rapid lifting, extension and rotation to be carried out simultaneously. The computer system also

monitors various safety devices on the ladder. As one of the world's leading turntable ladder manufacturers, Metz has supplied over 2,000 separate aerial fire engines with rescue heights of 18–53m/60–174ft to many fire brigades around the world. These have been mounted on a variety of commercial chassis, including Seagrave, MAN, Mercedes, Scania and Volvo.

30M/100FT TURNTABLE LADDER	
Year	1937
Engine	Leyland 6-cylinder petrol
Power	115bhp
Transmission	4-speed manual
Features	midships-mounted pump

MILLS-TUI

Based at Rotorua, New Zealand, Mills-Tui has built a number of fire engines for the nationalized New Zealand Fire Service and Australian fire brigades. Its range includes compact rural water

■ LEFT *A Scania G94D-260/Mills Tui standard heavy water tender of the New Zealand Fire Service.*

■ BELOW *This Mills-Tui/Mitsubishi water tender and aerial ladder is on duty in South Australia.*

PUMPER	
Year	1986
Engine	6-cylinder diesel
Power	185bhp
Transmission	5-speed manual
Features	crew safety cab

tenders based on the Mitsubishi 4x4 chassis, standard water tenders in both 4x2 and 4x4 configurations using chassis such as Scania and Dennis, and airport foam and crash tenders on suitable commercial chassis. Mills-Tui has also built combination heavy pumps and aerial ladder units and hazardous-material units.

MITSUBISHI

■ BELOW *A compact Mitsubishi light pump and rescue tender.*

A commercial Tokyo-based truck manufacturer, Mitsubishi provides a number of suitable chassis for fire service use in Japan and several Asian and Middle Eastern countries. These include the Japanese fire service MWG 40 T model water tender, which is fitted with a crew cab to accommodate up to six firefighters, a 4,000-litre/

880-gallon water tank and a 2,270-litres/500-gallons-per-minute pump.

Mitsubishi also supply a compact narrow-width chassis for firefighting where ready access by normal-sized water tenders would be difficult. This fire engine carries a crew of four and a 1,900-litres/420-gallons-per-minute pump. A heavier Mitsubishi chassis is used to mount 20m/65ft Morita hydraulic platforms and other specialist vehicles such as Hong Kong Fire Service's command unit.

■ LEFT *The Japanese Fire Service run this Mitsubishi/Fuso water tender.*

■ BELOW *A Hong Kong Fire Service command unit on a Mitsubishi coach chassis.*

OTHER MAKES

■ MARTE

Marte Vehicles was established in 1964 in Weiler, Austria, and four years later built its first fire vehicle, a light pump on a Land Rover 110 chassis. The following year, 1969, saw the start of an agency for Ziegler fire engines, and by 1977 Marte had delivered its 100th fire engine.

Steady development continued and in 1982 came an agreement with the German company, Metz, to deliver their turntable ladders to fire brigades in Austria. Additional manufacturing capacity was added in 1986 and four years later, the 500-vehicle benchmark was passed. By 1994, Marte had built and delivered 700 fire engines and this was followed by a further development five years later of the company's production facilities.

Marte has developed a modular construction system for its fire engine manufacture which utilizes screw-jointed and bonded aluminium components together with special fibreglass reinforced plastics, to resist corrosion.

■ MORITA

Founded in 1907, Morita is the largest of the Japanese fire engine manufacturers. In recent years, its fire engine models have ranged from water tenders and airport foam/crash tenders, through to aerial ladders and Snorkel platforms.

The typical Morita water tender of the last decade is available on a number of commercial chassis, including Toyota, Hino, Isuzu and Mitsubishi. The MWG 40T model has a 2,270 litres/500 gallons per minute water pump, a 4,000-litre/880-gallon water tank, and a crew cab for six firefighters. Morita uses the same chassis style for its foam tenders.

Morita aerial ladders come in heights of 18–40m/60ft–130ft. They are usually mounted with the turntable at the rear of the chassis, European style, and have a fitted rescue cage. In addition most Morita aerial ladders have onboard firefighting water pumps, making them a totally independent unit.

The Morita fire engine range includes Snorkel platforms mounted on Hino, Isuzu, Mitsubishi or Toyota chassis. In the 1970s, Morita started to follow American practice by adding a high-powered water monitor at the top of the platform, capable of delivering up to 3,000 litres/660 gallons of water per minute at the upper levels of high-rise buildings.

■ MOORE ENGINEERING

Moore Engineering was founded over 20 years ago and has its manufacturing base near to Adelaide, South Australia. The company builds a range that includes pumps and rescue tenders.

■ MORRIS COMMERCIAL

Morris Commercial, a British manufacturer of light vans and lorries, never seriously turned its attention to fire engine production and only produced a small number to special order during the years between World Wars I and II. These were mostly built as pumping fire engines using the Morris CS 11/40F chassis powered by a 25hp 6-cylinder petrol engine. They carried an all-enclosed 2,270-litres/500-gallons-per-minute pump mounted on the rear platform of the fire engine body and a 10m/35ft extension ladder. During the 1930s, Morris provided the chassis for some Magirus 30m/100ft turntable ladders.

■ MOWAG

Originally a bodybuilding concern, Mowag began manufacturing vehicles in 1951. Based in Kreuzlingen, Switzerland, the company now manufactures fire engines alongside a range of military cross-country all-wheel drive vehicles. In addition to its own chassis, Mowag utilizes the US Dodge for a number of its fire engine applications. Mowag water tenders of the 1950s were available with a Dodge (Chrysler) 125 bhp 6-cylinder or V8 8-cylinder engine on a 4.5-ton, eight-man crew cab 4x2 chassis. Subsequent versions used a 4x4 Dodge chassis with a 210bhp V8 petrol engine and incorporated a 1,200-litre/264-gallon water tank and a 2,800 litres/600 gallons per minute rear-mounted water pump. Mowag was taken over by General Motors in 1999, but since that time have ceased production of fire engines.

■ BELOW *A Hino/Moore Engineering 4x4 light pump designed for rural firefighting and rescue.*

■ BELOW *This modern Morita 40m/130ft six-section aerial ladder is mounted on a Hino 6x4 chassis.*

NATIONAL FOAM

National Foam is an American company that specializes in a range of firefighting foam delivery systems and equipment, both fixed and vehicle-mounted. Based in Exton, Pennsylvania, the company is now part of the Kidde FireFighting

■ ABOVE *The 16.5m/54ft-squirt boom of this 1992 International/National Foam 6x4 foam tender projects foam into oil tanks.*

■ BELOW *Texaco Oil Refinery, Anacortes, Washington, own this 1975 4x4 General Motors/National Foam foam tender.*

FOAM TENDER	
Year	1975
Engine	V6 petrol
Power	230bhp
Transmission	manual
Features	4x4

international organization. National Foam have built a number of foam pumpers, aerials and tankers and are associated with the Feecon company and its airport crash rescue equipment and also with the Wirt Knox firefighting accessories firm. National Foam are an acknowledged world leader in foam-based solutions.

NISSAN

The Nissan Company of Kawaguchi, Japan, provides many chassis for Japanese fire engines, including those of Tokyo's fire brigade, which is one of the largest in the world. In the early 1950s, the first Nissan F380 truck chassis were used for open-cab pumpers. These had a 6-cylinder, 85bhp, 3.6-litre petrol engine and a manual 4-speed gearbox. In the 1960s the Japanese fire services used the Nissan Patrol 4x4 as a light emergency-response vehicle. Modern-day Nissan fire engines include the tandem-axle 10-ton models in use in Tokyo as foam tenders.

■ RIGHT *Used by Dubai's fire service as a fast first-attendance vehicle, this Nissan 4x4 is designed to arrive at an incident before the full-sized fire engines. It carries the officer in charge of the station, two breathing-apparatus wearers and hydraulic rescue equipment for use at road accidents. Another passenger is the duty electrician from the local electricity company, who disconnects the electricity supply to any premises involved in fire.*

■ LEFT *This Nissan Diesel/Morita 6x4 32m/105ft turntable ladder is in service with Abu Dhabi Fire Brigade, United Arab Emirates. It has an inbuilt fire pump to provide an independent water supply to the ladder monitor.*

■ RIGHT *This German Fire Service c.1955 Opel Blitz/Metz light pump carries a front-mounted water pump.*

■ BELOW RIGHT *A 1940 Opel Blitz TSF light pump is painted in wartime livery.*

OPEL

Opel fire engines have a long history that predates World War II, when the company produced a large number of lightweight pumping and rescue fire engines at its base in Brandenburg, Germany. In preparation for war, Opel manufactured large numbers of special airfield tenders for use by the Luftwaffe, using several 3-ton 4x4 foam tenders and water tanker versions built on the Blitz chassis.

After World War II, Opel was re-established at Russelheim, and in the early 1950s the Blitz series was based on the 1.75-ton 330C model with several subsequent versions. The model introduced in 1960 was based on the first Opel semi-forward control chassis.

The 1970 2-ton version with a five-man crew cab with a 2.5-litre, 6-cylinder engine continued this style of lightweight multi-purpose fire engine.

BLITZ	
Year	1970
Engine	6-cylinder petrol
Power	2.5-litre
Transmission	4-speed manual
Features	5-man crew cab

Opel faded from the fire engine scene in the mid-1970s, when it ceased production of light trucks suitable for use as fire and rescue vehicles.

OSHKOSH

The headquarters of the Oshkosh Truck Corporation is in Oshkosh, Wisconsin, USA. Since its foundation in 1917 Oshkosh has built a range of heavy-duty all-wheel drive trucks. Since World War II, it has tended to specialize in heavy haulage trucks, including those for the military, all designed to operate in extreme weather conditions. So it is not surprising that in their airport foam and crash tenders, Oshkosh manufacture some of the world's largest fire engines for military, municipal airport and civil fire brigade use.

The M-23 airport foam/crash tender is Oshkosh's biggest fire engine. This gigantic vehicle is powered by twin Detroit Diesel engines, which provide a massive 984bhp. Twin automatic transmissions provide drive to the eight wheels. The M-23 carries 22,700 litres/5,000 gallons of water plus 1,950 litres/430 gallons of foam concentrate. Its fire

■ ABOVE *A 1999 Oshkosh T1-3000 6x6 foam tender carries 1,900 litres/420 gallons of foam concentrate.*

pump produces approximately 11,300 litres/2,500 gallons per minute to the roof-mounted monitor. All-up weight of the M-23 is 65 tons, but despite this the vehicle can reach its maximum speed of 80kmh/50mph in 55 seconds.

The M-15 Oshkosh is very similar in layout and style to the M-23 but the

smaller fire pump produces 4,100 litres/900 gallons per minute. It carries an 18,000-litre/4,000-gallon water tank and 2,300 litres/515 gallons of foam concentrate. Oshkosh built over 50 M-15s for the US Air Force, where the model was designated P-15. Some P-15s have front and rear-mounted foam turrets. The water turrets mounted on the front bumper of the M-series keep burning fuel away from the crashed aircraft and rescue scene.

■ LEFT *The 8,200-litres/1,800-gallons-per-minute pump on this giant 1978 Oshkosh M-15 8x8 foam tender draws on 18,000 litres/4,000 gallons of water and 2,300 litres/515 gallons of foam concentrate.*

The T-6 series is a 4x4 foam/crash tender with a 492bhp diesel engine that can reach 80kmh/50mph in 45 seconds. The 6x6 T-12 version has a larger water tank holding 13,600 litres/3,000 gallons. Some T-series Oshkosh models have a roof-mounted water tower with a spear toll that is capable of penetrating an aeroplane's fuselage to deliver water spray or foam inside.

Oshkosh rapid intervention vehicles (RIVs) are fast-response, 110kmh/70mph airport fire engines designed to get to a fire or accident scene ahead of the heavy foam/crash tenders. They have a powerful firefighting attack with a 2,270 litres/500 gallons per minute roof turret and a bumper turret. Most RIVs also have a dry-powder capacity.

Oshkosh has also built a range of aerial ladders and snorkels (boomed hydraulic platforms) based on the Oshkosh A and L series chassis. The L series chassis has a very low overall height of 1.8m/6ft from the road surface, which enables the ladders to be constructed with a low profile. This means they can negotiate low bridges and get to work in streets and within the curtilage of premises where headroom is restricted. The L series has the V6 Detroit Diesel engine developing 335bhp with automatic transmission.

■ RIGHT *A US Air Force Oshkosh P-15 8x8 foam tender sports two roof-mounted foam turrets. This vehicle ranks among the largest fire engines in the world.*

PEMFAB

In 1971, a firm entitled Imperial Fire Apparatus first started to build fire engines on a custom cab in conjunction with another company, Truck Cab Manufacturers of Cincinnati, Ohio. Four years later, Imperial Fire Apparatus was purchased by Pemberton Fabricators, and the name PemFab first appeared on American fire engines. During the next two decades, PemFab constructed a number of fire engines on custom chassis in the Pacemaker series and in the early 1980s, also introduced a new concept of wedge-shaped cab designs subsequently used on PemFab Premier, Royale, Sovereign, and Imperial models. The company ceased trading in 1996.

■ ABOVE *Skagit County Fire Department, Big Lake, Washington, operate this 1981 Emergency One/Pemfab pumper. It incorporates an 8,000-litres/1,750-gallons-per-minute pump and a 2,270-litre/500-gallon water tank.*

PETERBILT

Founded in 1938 by T Peterman, a logger, who was used to adapting and rebuilding army trucks for his own industry, the Peterbilt company grew out of the purchase of the assets of the defunct Waukesha Motor Company, with the primary purpose of custom-building logging trucks. In the first year Peterman delivered 14 trucks and in the second he had increased capacity to 82. During World War II the company supplied government contracts for heavy-duty trucks and was in a prime position to take a share of the market when war

ceased. Peterman died in 1945 and the assets were sold to a management group from the company. The company was put up for sale in 1958 when it was acquired by Kenworth, a competitor. In 1960 the company moved to Newark, California, and in 1969 a second plant was built in

■ ABOVE *Built in 1993, this huge Peterbilt/Custom Fire rescue tender serves in Canada.*

Tennessee, to cope with demand. In 1975 the Canadian Peterbilt opened for manufacture and in 1983 a further site was opened in Texas.

PIERCE

■ BELOW *A Delaware-based 2001 Kenworth/Pierce pumper awaits a call-out.*

The Pierce Company was founded in 1913 in Wisconsin, USA, when it was first engaged in making a variety of taxis and carriages. It constructed its first fire engine in the late 1940s, and was one of the first manufacturers to use aluminium widely in the vehicle-building process. Pierce developed a wide range of fire engines, from mini-pumpers to larger conventional American pumpers, rescue and crash tenders, water tankers and various aerial ladders and platforms.

The Ford L series, Chevrolet, Dodge and GMC chassis were used for many Pierce mini-pumpers, whilst the Ford C series or Duplex models formed the base for their Suburban series pumpers,

which were designed for urban firefighting and rescue. The later Pierce Arrow pumper range offered pumping capacities of 3,400–6,800 litres/ 750–1,500 gallons with a choice of

2,270-litre/500-gallon or 3,400-litre/ 750-gallon water tanks.

Pierce's aerial range includes the Squirt water tower, a 23m/75ft tower ladder with a 4,500 litres/1,000 gallons per minute nozzle; 32m/105ft aerials on tandem axle chassis; and 26m/85ft and 29m/95ft Snorkels. A number of Pierce aerials have been specially mounted on the low-line Oshkosh chassis to allow access into confined space in urban areas.

■ BELOW *This 1988 Superior/Pierce Dash foam tender is equipped with a 23m/75ft Telesquirt boom.*

RESCUE TENDER	
Year	1979
Engine	6-cylinder diesel
Power	275hp
Transmission	4-speed automatic
Features	wide range of power tools

PIERREVILLE

The Canadian fire engine manufacturer Pierreville Fire Trucks was founded in 1968 at Saint-François-du-Lac, Quebec. Its origins can be traced to the time when five sons of the Thibault family, which then owned the long-standing Thibault fire engine company, decided to start an independent manufacturing operation not far from the family headquarters.

Considerable success soon followed for Pierreville. Only ten years after its inauguration, when measured by the number of vehicles actually sold and with an order book worth C$8 million, the company could claim to be the

largest fire engine builder in Canada. By then it had developed a large factory base and at one stage employed 150 staff building pumpers and aerial ladders, not just for all the major Canadian fire departments and many smaller ones, but for a number of American fire departments as well.

However, Pierreville ceased trading in 1985, but soon afterwards most of its

assets and orders were assumed by several members of the Thibault family who formed a company that traded under the name of Camions Incendie Phoenix. This offshoot of Pierreville continued to build a number of various fire engines for eastern Canadian fire departments until 1992 when it too ceased trading and finally disappeared from the fire vehicle scene.

■ ABOVE RIGHT *Vancouver Fire Department, British Columbia, Canada, took delivery of this Imperial/Pierreville pumper in 1974.*

■ RIGHT *The University of British Columbia Fire Department, Canada, operate this 1979 Scot Pierreville 30m/ 100ft rear-mount aerial ladder.*

PIRSCH

■ BELOW *This 1977 Pirsch pumper serves in Blaine, Minnesota.*

Peter Pirsch was a volunteer fireman in the 1880s who took to constructing wooden extension ladders for his own fire department before building some early motorized pumpers. He founded

PUMPER	
Year	1952
Engine	6-cylinder petrol
Power	127bhp
Transmission	4-speed manual
Features	enclosed front cab

■ RIGHT *Carrying 2,270 litres/500 gallons of water, this 1970 Pirsch pump delivers 5,700 litres/1,250 gallons per minute.*

his fire engine company in Wisconsin, USA, in 1900, since which time the Pirsch name has become synonymous with aerial ladders throughout America. The company went on to develop aerial-ladder technology with the pioneering use of aluminium alloys in the construction of ladder sections. It produced the first all-powered American aerial ladder in 1930.

Pirsch aerial ladders include tractor-drawn versions and have either rear or centre-mounted models with up to 30m/100ft working height. A number of twin-boom Pirsch 26m/85ft Snorkels are also in service in addition to the Pirsch range of pumpers with midships pumps, twin hose reels and top-mounted pump controls. Some Pirsch mini-pumpers have been supplied on a Chevrolet chassis.

OTHER MAKES

■ PRAGA

For many years Praga chassis were used for many fire engines built in former Czechoslovakia for use in East Europe. After World War II the Praga A150 1.5-ton truck chassis was regularly used for light fire tenders. The Praga A150 had a 4-cylinder, 55bhp petrol engine, and, unusually, independent front suspension. The V3S series 6x6 heavy chassis with an air-cooled Tatra diesel engine formed the basis for a number of airfield foam/crash tenders and some pumping fire engines. Many Praga fire engines had bodywork constructed by the Czech Korosa company.

PLASTISOL

Plastisol BV is a Dutch company based in Wanroij, Holland, which specializes in fibreglass reinforced polyester construction. The company designs and manufactures crew cabs and bodywork for fire engine use, using a range of commercial chassis including those of Chevrolet, General Motors and Dodge.

In 2002, Plastisol manufactured the tilting one-piece crew cabs and bodywork of 107 new pumping fire engines for the London Fire Brigade. These fire engines are based on a Mercedes Benz Atego 1325F chassis, and a feature of the London pumps are their water and foam tanks which are included in the body core structure.

Among some of Plastisol's other fire service general bodywork applications

are superstructures for airport rescue tenders, demountable foam containers, and foam trailers with concentrate capacities ranging from 3,000 litres/660 gallons to 16,000 litres/3,524 gallons.

■ ABOVE *A 9,000-litre/2,000-gallon water tender on a Volvo chassis with Plastisol body.*

■ BELOW *A Scania 124c 420/Carmichael Viper airport foam tender with Plastisol body.*

PUMP	
Year	2003
Engine	6-cylinder
Power	326hp
Transmission	automatic
Features	modular locker stowage

QUALITY

Having built its first fire engines in 1962 for US fire brigades, Quality has continued to grow steadily and develop its model range to include a variety of pumpers, rescue trucks and aerial ladders.

The Americana pumper can be built with up to 50 different equipment compartment configurations and to any length. The Avenger pumper has a short-wheelbase chassis with water tank capacities of 4,500–5,700 litres/1,000–1,250 gallons. The aluminium body of the Colonial model is constructed of only nine extrusions, whilst the Liberty can serve as a rescue pumper with 6cu m/220cu ft of equipment-storage space. The 2002 Volunteer model is an

open-cab pumper with a body built of tubular steel and stainless steel plate. Quality's aerial ladder platform models, known as the Independence range, have working heights of 15–33m/50–110ft.

In the 1990s the ownership of the Quality fire engine company was acquired by Spartan Motors Inc, and in 2003 Quality became part of the new Crimson Fire company.

■ ABOVE *Hayward Fire Department, California, run this 1992 Spartan/Quality pumper with a 9,000-litres/2,000-gallons-per-minute pump.*

■ RIGHT *This 1999 6x4 Quality/E-One 30.4m/100ft aerial ladder is in service with Marrero Harvey Fire Department, Louisiana.*

■ BELOW *This mid-1980s Renault turbo water tender serves in Belgium.*

RENAULT

French company Renault has had an increasing presence in the European fire engine market, especially since it acquired Dodge (UK) in the 1980s and replaced the Dodge logo on a number of water tenders, emergency tenders and aerial ladders with the Renault logo. The Renault G13TC, G16C, G17C, the M230 Midliner and S66C chassis were among those that featured in British fire engine renewal programmes in the early 1990s, with large sections of several fire brigade pumping fleets now carrying the Renault badge.

G300 RAIL RESCUE UNIT	
Year	1995
Engine	6-cylinder diesel
Power	300hp
Transmission	manual
Features	underslung rail wheels

A somewhat unusual Renault application in the UK is that of two railway support vehicles built in 1995 on a G300 tandem-axle chassis to attend emergency calls to the three-mile-long Severn Rail Tunnel near Bristol. They carry heavy rescue equipment and have rail wheels that allow them to run on the railway lines in the tunnel.

The Renault 95-130, 4x4 heavy-duty, all-terrain vehicle is used in France for forest firefighting, and a number of Renault chassis have been used in Belgium as the base for 30m/100ft turntable ladders. A number of Renault T35 vans have been converted for use as incident support units and breathing set tenders, which attend large-scale firefighting and rescue incidents.

■ ABOVE *Incidents in the UK's Severn Tunnel are attended by this Avon Fire Brigade Renault G800 6x4 rail-rescue unit.*

■ RIGHT *This 1988 Renault S56 4x4 hose layer is permanently based at Heathrow (London) Airport.*

REYNOLDS BOUGHTON

Based in Devon, England, Reynolds Boughton has produced a wide range of firefighting and rescue vehicles for service in both the UK and overseas. The company is particularly well known for its work on the Pathfinder airfield crash tender introduced in 1971. This was built on a Reynolds Boughton 6x6 chassis using a General Motors V16 supercharged 2-stroke diesel engine

■ LEFT *The high-pressure pump of this British Army Fire Service Reynolds Boughton RB44, 4x4 light pump/foam tender feeds two hose reels. This tender carries 450 litres/100 gallons of water and has a front-mounted winch.*

PATHFINDER	
Year	1971
Engine	General Motors V16 diesel
Power	600bhp
Transmission	automatic
Features	Pyrene foam system

rated in excess of 600bhp. The Pathfinder foam system was developed in conjunction with Pyrene, the British foam specialists. Its remote-controlled roof-mounted monitor could project a foam jet 75m/250ft at 61,300 litres/ 13,500 gallons per minute.

In addition to airport vehicles, Reynolds Boughton continues to design and build many types of fire engines, including water tenders and various specialist vehicles.

ROSENBAUER

Having built its first fire engine in 1866, Rosenbauer International, based in Leonding, Austria, is a long established company. Today it is one of the largest global exporters of most types of firefighting and rescue vehicles and equipment to fire brigade customers throughout the world. Almost 1,300 employees are based at the company's eight European production plants, which together with six manufacturing centres in America and Asia currently produce over 14,000 vehicles per year.

For many years Rosenbauer has used a wide range of chassis makes and types, including Steyr, Mercedes, Renault, OM, Ford, Scania, Chevrolet, Henschel and Faun models. A typical early 1950s Rosenbauer water tender for the Austrian fire service was built on a German V8 4x4 Ford chassis with a 1,500-litre/330-gallon water tank and a front-mounted 1,500 litres/330 gallons per minute front-mounted pump. The crash/foam tender delivered to Vienna Airport in the same period was mounted on a Saurer 6GAF-LL 4x4 diesel engine

■ LEFT *A late 1970s Magirus Deutz/Rosenbauer 4x4 water tender on duty with Crete Fire Service.*

■ LEFT *Bruges Fire Brigade, Belgium, operate this Renault turbo/Rosenbauer 6x4 foam/water tender. Lengths of hard suction hose are stored amidships.*

chassis with a 4,000-litre/880-gallon water tank.

In the 1960s Rosenbauer produced a number of light water tenders on the semi-forward-control Opel Blitz 1961 chassis for service in Germany. Their basic firefighting equipment included a light portable 800-litres/176-gallons-per-minute pump. In 1972 Rosenbauer

built a 26m/85ft 3-boom hydraulic platform on a Steyr 1,290 chassis with a 230bhp diesel engine. In 1974 it pioneered a demountable equipment pod system using flatbed lorries as prime movers.

■ BELOW *A 1988 Oshkosh/Rosenbauer 8x8 foam tender at a Wisconsin airport, USA.*

■ BELOW *Onboard firefighting equipment carried by this German Fire Service 1980 Magirus Deutz/Rosenbauer HF16 water tender includes an electronically controlled pump.*

■ RIGHT *Stationed at Padderborn Airport, Germany, this MAN F2000/Rosenbauer Buffalo 9000 6x6 airport foam tender is powered by a V10 600hp turbo diesel engine.*

A recent model from Rosenbauer's considerable range, which makes use of many chassis makes, includes the small firefighting TSF vehicle built on a Mercedes-Benz 414 series 4x4 chassis with a 4-cylinder, 143bhp petrol engine. The TSF carries a crew of eight and has a portable 1,300-litres/286-gallons-per-minute pump.

Another mid-range fire engine is the forest firefighting tender, on a Toyota Hi-Lux 4x4 chassis carrying a 2,000-litre/440-gallon water tank and 200 litres/44 gallons of foam concentrate agent. The larger PLF6000 dry-powder tender for petrochemical plants utilizes a MAN 6x4 chassis with a 264bhp diesel engine. This specialized

■ BELOW *Köln/Bonn Airport, Germany, operates this 1985 Rosenbauer 4x4 foam tender fitted with roof-mounted monitors.*

fire engine carries two tanks, each containing 3,000kg/6,600lb of dry powder, which, when activated, is expelled by a nitrogen gas system at rates of 25–50kg/55–110lb per second.

Some of Rosenbauer's largest fire engines are airport foam tenders. These models include the FLF Panther range, constructed on either a Freightliner or MAN chassis in 4x4, 6x6 or 8x8 configurations. One 8x8 Panther version is built on a MAN 38,100 DFAEG chassis with 1,000hp diesel engine driving through an automatic transmission, which gives an approximate top speed of 140kmh/87mph, with 0–80kmh/50mph acceleration in 24 seconds. A three-man steel safety cab is fitted. The pump output is 7,000 litres/1,540 gallons per minute with the roof-mounted monitor capable of discharging 6,000 litres/1,320 gallons

per minute with a throw of 90m/295ft, while a front-mounted monitor produces 800 litres/175 gallons per minute. The Panther also has seven low-level nozzles. The water tank capacity is 12,500 litres/2,750 gallons and the foam concentrate tank carries 800 litres/175 gallons. The all-up weight of this Panther is 38.5 tons.

OTHER MAKES

■ RK AERIALS
RK Manufacturing was founded by Rob and Pam Kreikemeier in Fremont, Nebraska, USA, in 1988 with a modest 465sq m/5,000sq ft building and three employees. Since then, the company has grown rapidly. Within eight years, RK's manufacturing area had quadrupled, producing an annual output of 12 aerial ladders. Within two years, the production facility had doubled to cover 3,700sq m/40,000sq ft, and the staff was up to 35. In January 2000, RK Aerials joined the Rosenbauer America Group enterprise.

RK Aerials now builds ladders in 18m/60ft, 23m/75ft and 33.2m/109ft lengths. The aerial platform models come in 26m/85ft and 31.7m/104ft versions. All RK aerials are available as mid or rear mounts.

S&S FIRE APPARATUS

American company S&S Fire Apparatus began operating in the early 1980s as an independent fire engine manufacturer. It has offices in Fairmount, Indiana, and Keller, Texas.

The company is an innovative and pioneering leader in the use of stainless steel for fire vehicle construction. It has steadily developed its fire vehicle range with an impressive 100 per cent growth during the past decade. The range now includes the Indure stainless steel pumpers, SS-T and Infinity III (elliptical) series tanker/pumpers, and Highland mini-pumpers. S & S have recently acquired the Attack 1 fire apparatus product line including high-

■ ABOVE *A 1997 Peterbilt/S&S tanker of Hempfield Fire Department, Pennsylvania.*

strength lightweight bodies, and the resulting S&S Quick Attack light brush fire engines, which have inbuilt quality and performance. Hundreds of S&S off-road fire engines are operating with the US Forest Service and Bureau of Land Management and the company's severe-duty vehicles are well proven in their wildland and brush firefighting capacity.

■ BELOW *Frankford Fire Department's, Delaware, Ford/S&S light pumper.*

SAULSBURY

The American fire engine builder Saulsbury Fire Rescue Company has built up an enviable reputation for the design and manufacture of rescue tenders, both compact models and those mounted on bigger chassis to allow for a larger equipment payload. Saulsbury rescue tenders carry a vast range of high-powered lifting, cutting and other specialized equipment that is often needed to deal with a variety of non-fire emergencies.

Rescue tenders are built to the specific needs of individual fire

departments. For example, Philadelphia Fire Department has a tandem-axle Saulsbury dedicated as a heavy-rescue unit with a crew of one officer and five firefighters. Another Saulsbury tandem-

axle heavy rescue model provides the facility of a mid-chassis-mounted 13-ton crane with hydraulically extended arms.

The Saulsbury Fire Rescue Company was acquired by Emergency One in 1998.

6x4 HEAVY RESCUE TENDER	
Year	1992
Engine	6-cylinder diesel
Power	350hp
Transmission	4-speed automatic
Features	heavy-duty rescue equipment

■ ABOVE *A Delaware-based 1999 Saulsbury heavy rescue unit stands by.*

■ LEFT *Hockessin Fire Company, Delaware, own this smart 1999 Saulsbury tanker.*

SAVIEM

In the years following World War II, Saviem, based in Seine, France, constructed a number of chassis for fire engines widely used throughout France, including water tenders, industrial foam tenders and airport foam/crash tenders.

SM10 FOAM TENDER	
Year	1971
Engine	6-cylinder diesel
Power	170bhp
Transmission	4-speed manual
Features	remote-controlled monitor

These included the JL23 chassis for heavy water tenders with a pump output around 2,270 litres/500 gallons per minute, and a typical airport tender built in the early 1960s on the Saviem TZ21-N 6x6 chassis. This model had a 6-cylinder 180bhp petrol engine, but, unusually at the time, the fire-water pump was powered by a separate

■ ABOVE *A Renault/Saviem 6x4 rear-mount hydraulic platform is ready for the next call-out.*

Chevrolet power plant, nowadays a common feature on airport fire tenders. In later years, Saviem fire engines became progressively part of the expanding Renault commercial vehicle division.

SAXON SANBEC

One of the UK's major fire engine bodybuilders, Saxon Sanbec's manufacturing base is located at its expanding Sandbach premises in Cheshire, England. The company began operation in 1982, soon after the demise of the Cheshire Fire Engineering Company, formerly part of the fire engine bodybuilding division of ERF (an acronym of the founder's name).

Saxon Sanbec has grown impressively over the past two decades, to design and

RESCUE PUMP	
Year	1990
Engine	diesel
Power	6-litre
Transmission	5-speed manual
Features	range of rescue equipment

■ BELOW *One of the London Fire Brigade's stylish 1990 Volvo FL6.14/Saxon rescue pumps idles in a park.*

supply a large number of fire engines in use throughout the UK's fire brigades. They include water tenders, rescue tenders, aerial ladders, control units and a number of other special-use vehicles. Saxon Sanbec fire engines are based on a variety of commercial chassis, including those of Dennis, Dodge, Mercedes, Scania and Volvo.

■ BELOW *A pair of Saxon water tenders – on the left, a Mercedes 814L and on the right, a Mercedes 1124F.*

■ BELOW *This odd-looking three-wheeled 1939 Scammell pulled a 2,160-litres/475-gallons-per-minute Scammell trailer pump.*

■ BOTTOM *A British Royal Air Force Scammell/Carmichael 4x4 foam tender attends a fire engine rally.*

SCAMMELL

Scammell Motors of Watford, England, was already a significant builder of commercial trucks and military vehicles when it built its first of a series of fire engines in 1933. This was for the local fire brigade and was based on their F7B chassis with 4-cylinder, 85bhp petrol engine, a 1,800 litres/400 gallons per minute midships pump and a 180-litre/40-gallon water tank. An unusual feature of this Scammell was the fitting of an electric heater in the engine cooling system to keep the water sufficiently warm to ensure immediate starting in

MOUNTAINEER 4X4	
Year	1950
Engine	8-cylinder petrol
Power	150bhp
Transmission	4-speed manual
Features	foam tender

cold weather conditions. The Scammell model F6, which featured a lowered dropframe chassis and 6-speed manual gearbox, was introduced in 1935.

A completely different kind of fire engine was the wartime 6-ton Utility MH6 mechanical horse three-wheeled model introduced in 1939. This carried a two-man crew and had a 1,600-litre/

350-gallon water tank, a transverse-mounted 110-litres/25-gallons-per-minute pump, a hose and a short ladder. The MH6 was also capable of pulling a Scammell 2,160 litres/475 gallons per minute trailer pump. After World War II, Scammell heavy 4x4 and 6x6 chassis were used for a number of overseas foam tenders going into service in Venezuela.

SCANIA

Scania is one of the world's largest manufacturers of heavy trucks and buses, having no fewer than 11 factories in five countries. Founded originally in Sweden in 1891, Scania celebrated its millionth truck off the production line in 2000. Originally trading as Scania-Vabis, the company merged in 1969 with Saab to become Saab-Scania. From then on the truck and bus division simply became known as Scania.

Scania fire engines came into widespread general use outside Scandinavia during the 1970s. Until then the standard Scania-Vabis Swedish water tender had a 3,000-litre/660-gallon water tank with a pump capable of maximum output of 2,500 litres/

550 gallons per minute. In 1970 Scania also provided the chassis for some of the first of the modern-style emergency tenders for the Swedish fire service. These used the normal control L80 chassis with the Scania DS8 6-cylinder 190bhp turbocharged diesel engines. Some of these emergency tenders were among the first to incorporate a hydraulic lifting arm, now a relatively normal fitting on fire engines used for a range of non-fire rescue work.

Once the first Scania chassis started to be used for fire engine construction in Europe, the Scania badge rapidly became visible in many fire brigades. The first Scania fire engines in the UK were turntable ladders in the early 1980s, and were soon followed by the first Scania water tenders, mostly on the G92M 4x2 chassis.

The current Scania fire engine range includes the standard water tender built on the P94 GB 4x2 chassis, which can provide a normal water tank capacity of up to 4,000 litres/880 gallons. The P94 is powered by the DSC9 260bhp diesel engine with automatic transmission and has a pump capable of output of up to 3,000 litres/660 gallons per minute. This water tender weighs in at just over 18 tons. A 4x4 version, the P124 CB model is available with the DSC12 diesel engine producing 400bhp. Many such modern Scania chassis are also in widespread use as emergency/rescue tenders, foam tenders, water tankers and prime movers. In addition, the Scania P124 6x4 360 26-ton chassis forms the base for a range of aerial platforms and turntable ladders and is powered by a 360bhp diesel engine.

L80	
Year	1971
Engine	8-cylinder diesel
Power	190bhp
Transmission	5-speed manual
Features	normal control cab

■ ABOVE *This 1926 Scania-Vabis pump carries a 15m/50ft removable wheeled escape ladder. A lot of equipment is stowed on the running board.*

■ RIGHT *A 1999 Scania 94D 260/John Dennis Coachbuilders water tender of Cambridgeshire Fire and Rescue Service, England.*

▲ SEAGRAVE

■ BELOW *The coiled hose draped across the bonnet of this preserved 1933 Seagrave 6B pumper is ready to connect to a street hydrant. This fire engine was owned by Gustine Fire Department, California.*

One of the best-known American fire engine manufacturers, Seagrave is particularly renowned for its long experience and expertise with aerial ladder design. The company was founded in Michigan by Frederick Seagrave in 1881 to build simple ladders for fruit-picking work, but before long Seagrave was approached by a local fire department to try his hand at constructing a wheeled firefighting platform for transporting ladders to fires. Soon Seagrave was building considerable numbers of horse-drawn wooden ladders and the company moved to larger premises at Columbus, Ohio.

The largest of the Seagrave aerial ladders reached up to 26m/85ft, but required considerable hand-winding efforts by at least four men. Driven by competition from other fire engine builders, notably American LaFrance, in

around 1900 Seagrave developed a successful system using coiled springs to assist the extension of the aerial ladder. In 1935 it produced the world's first all-welded alloy-steel ladder and soon after, the first fully hydraulically operated aerial ladder, where all operations were powered by oil pressure.

Meanwhile Seagrave also began building motorized pumpers for many US fire departments, and by the start of

World War I had pioneered a number of technical developments. These included the centrifugal water pump, which was much more efficient than rotary and piston types, and engine cooling systems, which are vital when pumping for hours at a time. Seagrave continued to develop its range of aerials and pumpers, with the characteristic Seagrave-snout bonnets being a feature of their post-war fire engines.

■ BELOW *A 1992 Seagrave 32m/105ft mid-mount rear-steer aerial ladder of Mounds View Fire Department, Minnesota.*

■ BELOW *This 1989 Seagrave JR 30m/100ft rear-mount aerial ladder is in service with Stanwood Fire Department, Washington.*

■ BELOW MIDDLE *A 6x4 1988 Seagrave JE pumper of Truckee Meadows Fire Department, Nevada, stands at the ready in the station yard.*

In 1964 Seagrave was acquired by the FWD Corporation, makers of heavy-duty trucks for both public and military use, and soon afterwards Seagrave moved to FWD's headquarters at Clintonville, Wisconsin, where Seagrave continued to develop a range of aerials, ladders and pumpers. Some longer tractor-drawn articulated aerials came with a rear-steer axle controlled by a tillerman.

A typical Seagrave 30m/100ft rear-mount aerial ladder, such as those in service in New York Fire Department, was powered by a V6 Detroit Diesel engine with 350hp and 4-speed automatic transmission. The New York aerials weighed in at 14.5 tons. Seagrave pumpers were available with an 8,000-litres/1,750-gallons-per-minute pump and a number of features including low-line cab floor and twin hose reels.

■ BELOW *Newark Fire Department, Delaware, operate this colossal 1987 Seagrave 30m/100ft mid-mount rear-steer aerial ladder.*

SHAND MASON

The origins of Shand Mason can be traced back to 1774, when James Phillips, a London engineer, started building manual pumps. His company was acquired by the larger engineering firm of WJ Tilley, and in 1851 the growing business adopted the name of Shand Mason. By then the London-based company was building some solid and reliable horse-drawn manual pumps, but in 1856 it produced the first steam-driven fire pumper.

At the 1862 fire engine trials held during the Great Exhibition in London's Hyde Park, England, a Shand Mason easily won the small fire engine class, while its great rival, Merryweather, won the large class. Shand Mason steam engines used a shorter stroke in both their single and later 2-cylinder models and were generally more technically advanced than those of Merryweather. The company won significant orders from both the UK and abroad, and produced large numbers of fire engines from its London factory at Blackfriars.

In 1863, Shand Mason's output was 17 steam fire engines, of which two were destined for the London Fire Engine Establishment, while the remaining 15 went overseas to fire brigades in New Zealand, India, Russia and Poland. Soon after self-propelled steam fire

STEAM PUMP	
Year	1890
Engine	2-cylinder steam
Power	15hp
Transmission	horse-drawn
Features	1,589lpm/350gpm output

engines first appeared in America in 1867, both Shand Mason and Merryweather produced similar models. Shand Mason's attempts at a self-propelled steam fire engine were never successful, however, leaving Merryweather to capitalize on and steadily monopolize the steam fire engine scene. Despite the arrival of the petrol engine for fire brigade use in the early 1900s, Shand Mason doggedly stuck to steam power. The company's inevitable decline came in 1922, when the remnants of the once proud world-leading fire engine manufacturer were acquired by Merryweather, its long-standing competitor.

SHELVOKE AND DREWRY

Shelvoke and Drewry of Letchworth, England, was originally a builder of municipal vehicles for local authority use. In the 1970s the company turned its attention to the fire brigade market with a range of chassis types. These included the CX 4x4 for airport fire and rescue use, using the Rolls-Royce B81 235bhp engine with automatic gearbox. Until 1986 the company also built a number of water tenders and turntable/aerial ladders as well as several specials for various UK fire brigades. These Shelvoke and Drewry fire engines were based on the WX and

heavier WY chassis but despite their innovative crew cab, few fire trucks of this make have survived in active operational service with fire brigades.

■ ABOVE *This 1978 model Shelvoke and Drewry/Cheshire Fire Engineering water tender utilized a new four-door cab designed specifically for fire engine use.*

SIDES

The French Sides company originated in 1951 and has steadily grown to become a very large manufacturer of fire engines for all types of operational use, including municipal, industrial and aviation fire brigades. Now part of the Kidde Group, the company has its manufacturing base at Saint Nazaire, where 73 per cent of fire engine output is destined for export.

The vehicle range includes first-attack units, pump water tenders, forest fire tenders, rescue tenders, industrial fire engines which use dry powder, foam and gases, and airport tenders both large and small. A typical

water tender is the VPI first-attack unit, built on a Renault S150.08/A4 4x2 chassis. It carries 1,000 litres/ 220 gallons of water and has a pump capacity of 1,000 litres/220 gallons per minute.

Sides airport fire engines are in service at over 200 airports worldwide.

■ LEFT *In service with the French military, this Sides 6x6 airport foam tender stands by on the taxiway of an air force base in France.*

One of the largest is the S3000 major foam crash tender model, mounted on a Sides 35,800 6x6 chassis. It has a 13,600-litre/3,000-gallon water tank and carries 1,600 litres/350 gallons of foam concentrate, together with 250kg/550lb of dry powder. The water pump has an output of 6,700 litres/1,475 gallons, while the roof-mounted dual monitor has a discharge rate of 6,000 litres/1,320 gallons per minute with a maximum reach of up to 85m/280ft. The Sides 3000 also features a front bumper-mounted monitor.

6x6 AIRPORT FOAM TENDER	
Year	1963
Engine	8-cylinder petrol
Power	330bhp
Transmission	6-speed manual
Features	high-output foam capacity

■ LEFT *This French military compact 4x4 Sides foam tender has a powerful roof monitor and a bumper-mounted winch.*

■ OPPOSITE *Norwich Airport, England, have this Gloster Saro/Simon Javelin 6x6 foam tender in operational use.*

■ BELOW *A 1990 Simon/Duplex/Grumman tanker in service with Odessa Fire Company, Delaware.*

SIMON

In 1963 Simon Engineering of Dudley, England, built the first British hydraulic platform for firefighting and rescue use. Simon's early platforms differed substantially from those of contemporary American makes through the use of three elevating booms rather than two. For more than two decades, the company delivered platforms to many British and overseas fire brigades.

The first Simon hydraulic platform, a SS65 model (20m/65ft) mounted on a Commer chassis, went into service in Monmouthshire Fire Brigade in 1963. Later Simon models included the DS50 (15m/50ft), SS70 (21m/70ft), SS85 (26m/85ft) and the SS263 (27.7m/91ft). Simon also produced a 15m/50ft telescopic arm mounted on a turntable with a high-discharge water monitor at the top. Known as the Simonitor, this could deliver up to 3,600 litres/ 800 gallons per minute at its head. The monitor could be remotely controlled from the ground or from the top of a

■ LEFT *The British Defence Fire Services have been supplied with several c.1980 Gloster Saro/Simon 4x4 Mk 10 foam/crash tenders, such as this example.*

■ LEFT *Derbyshire Fire and Rescue Service, England, run this 1990 Dennis F127/ Saxon/Simon ST240-S 24m/78ft aerial ladder platform.*

narrow ladder slung above the telescopic booms. Simon later developed an aerial ladder platform, which combined a telescopic boom with a hydraulic platform and a ladder that ranged alongside the variable length of the main boom. This series included the ALP 340 model, which was mounted on a suitable 3-axle chassis.

The Simon company was acquired by IVECO Magirus of Germany in 2000, after which the Simon aerial fire engine range was marketed under the Magirus name alone.

340 AERIAL LADDER PLATFORM

Year	1996
Engine	6-cylinder diesel
Power	310bhp
Transmission	automatic
Features	34m/111ft working height

■ ABOVE *In the 1990s Simon introduced a new aerial ladder platform, known as the 340. This demonstration model is built on a Mercedes 2435 6x4 chassis.*

■ BELOW *This magnificent 1988 Simon-Duplex/LTI 30m/100ft 6x4 rear-mount aerial ladder is in service with Fletcher Fire Department, North Carolina, USA.*

SKILLED EQUIPMENT MANUFACTURING

In 1996, the established Australian company Skilled Equipment joined forces with the Victoria Country Fire Authority, which had traditionally built its own fire engines for more than 40 years. The outcome was a joint arrangement to build fire engines, and one year later, Skilled Equipment Manufacturing was inaugurated.

Since then, the company have constructed a wide range of fire engines for various Australian fire brigades and a number of overseas customers. In 2000 the company acquired the interests of the Australian Fire Company and although production continued for a time at the latter's South Australian plant, from 2002 all manufacturing operations were concentrated at Skilled Equipment's premises at Ballarat.

■ ABOVE *One of a number of American LaFrance/Skilled Equipment Manufacturing pumpers delivered to Queensland Fire & Rescue Service in 2001.*

■ BELOW *In 2001 Western Australia Fire and Rescue received their second Scania P124G 360/Bronto F32/Skilled EM 8x4 32m/105ft aerial ladder platform.*

■ RIGHT *A*
Freightliner FL80/
Skilled Equipment
Manufacturing 6x4
Australian heavy
pumper of the
Metropolitan Fire
Brigade.

■ BELOW RIGHT
This Category 7
Mitsubishi light
tanker is one of 20
built by Skilled
Engineering
Manufacturing for
Australia's New
South Wales Fire
Service.

Apart from using a range of
commercial chassis, Skilled EM have
produced fire engines both large and
small for the Australian Fire Service for
operational use in city centres and at
incidents in the remote outback regions.
In 2001 Skilled EM delivered pumpers
to Queensland Fire and Rescue built
on an American LaFrance chassis,
quite an unusual combination. In
the same year, the company also
delivered 20 light tankers,
manufactured on a Mitsubishi Canter
4x4 chassis, for the New South Wales
Rural Fire Service; and a much larger
fire engine – a Scania P124 360/Bronto
32m/104ft aerial ladder platform, that
was delivered to Western Australia Fire
and Rescue.

■ BELOW *A*
Mitsibushi/Skilled
Equipment
Manufacturing
4x4 light pump
with rear crew cab.

124 8x4 ALP	
Year	2001
Engine	diesel
Power	360bhp
Transmission	automatic
Features	32m/105ft height

🚒 SMEAL

The Smeal Fire Apparatus Company began life in Snyder, Nebraska in 1964, when welder Don Smeal, a volunteer firefighter, was asked to repair the local fire department's fire engine. Don suggested that the fire board buy a new chassis so that he could build a unique fire engine. The resultant vehicle had an enclosed six-man crew cab, water tank, and 12.8m/42ft, two-section, hydraulically operated ladder. The new fire engine was so successful that the interest it generated heralded the birth of the Smeal company.

Nowadays, Smeal is recognized for its excellent engineering and workmanship across its wide range of pumpers, aerials and platforms. The

■ LEFT *A 2000 Spartan G/Smeal 16.8m/55ft pumper/ladder working in Ontario, Canada.*

■ BELOW LEFT *Skagit County Fire District, Allen, Washington, own this 1988 Ford C8000/Smeal 4,500-litres/1,000-gallons-per-minute pumper.*

■ BELOW *Vancouver Fire Department's 2001 Spartan Gladiator 6x4/Smeal 30m/100ft aerial ladder.*

PUMPER	
Year	2003
Engine	8-cylinder diesel
Power	370 bhp
Transmission	automatic
Features	combined urban/rural use

pumper range includes the Volunteer, Urban, and Freedom models, a compressed air foam version, custom and crossmount series.

During 2003, Smeal have delivered an interesting order for more than 20 multi-functional pumpers for Riverside County, California. These are to fulfil both urban and rural operational use and are based upon the Spartan Sierra chassis/cab with Cummins ISL 370hp engine and Allison automatic transmission. Water tanks with 2,270-

litre/500-gallon capacity are fitted and a 9,080-litres/2,000-gallons-per-minute pump provides a powerful firefighting attack with a 113-litre/25-gallon foam concentrate supply.

Smeal aerials are available in a number of heights ranging from 16.7m/55ft heavy duty to 38.1m/125ft heavy duty, with mid and rear-mount options on 4x4 and 6x4 chassis. Similarly, Smeal platforms are available in 25.9m/85ft heights through to 30.5m/100ft in mid and rear-mount models.

SNORKEL

Snorkel aerial fire engines first made an appearance on the American scene in 1968. Having noticed the locally-used small fruit-picking trucks, which had two elevating booms with a small basket at the top for the fruit picker, Chicago Fire Department commissioned the Missouri-based Pittman Manufacturing Company to build a 16.8m/55ft version. Based on a General Motors chassis for firefighting duties, it had a working platform at its head that was able to take several firefighters. The 5cm/2in diameter nozzle was capable of delivering water into the upper floors of a burning building at a rate of 5,500 litres/1,200 gallons per minute.

The prototype platform was so successful that Chigaco Fire Department ordered more of the same. Before long the Snorkel Fire Equipment Company had been formed at Elwood, Kansas, to manufacture hydraulically operated fire-fighting and rescue platforms 16.8–26m/55–85ft high. In some cases these were mounted on a suitable pumper chassis to produce a combination fire engine, able to pump water and work at height.

28M/85FT SNORKEL	
Year	1972
Engine	V8 diesel
Power	350bhp
Transmission	manual
Features	6x4

Modern Snorkels have electrical power in the platform for operating cutting tools together with a piped air supply for breathing sets. Further developments have been the intro-duction of a remote controlled nozzle to avoid firefighters having to work at the head of the booms, and a combination aerial ladder-telescopic water tower.

■ RIGHT *This 1987 23m/75ft Snorkel is based on a Spartan MS20/Van Pelt/FMC 6x4 chassis. It belongs to the City of Arroyo Grande Fire Department, in California.*

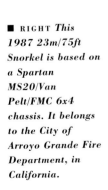

SPARTAN FIRE & EMERGENCY

Spartan Fire and Emergency was founded in 1973 and its manufacturing base is located at Spartanburg, South Carolina, USA. Its large range of fire engines, mostly on Pierce chassis, includes pumpers with 6,800-litre/1,500-gallon tanks and pumps with outputs of 2,270–9,000 litres/500–2,000 gallons per minute. Its extensive aerial ladder range includes 30m/100ft tractor-drawn models and Schwing water towers with articulated arms. Spartan also builds the Snozzle range of fire engines for industrial use. These vehicles have a hydraulic arm for those emergency

■ TOP *Storey County Fire Department, Nevada, operate this blue and white 1992 Spartan/HiTech pumper.*

■ RIGHT *This Delaware-based 1990 Spartan/4-Guys 6x4 tanker sports a highly polished stainless steel water tank.*

■ BELOW *A 1992 Spartan Gladiator/ Darley 6x4 pumper of Point Roberts Fire Rescue, Washington, has a 6,800-litres/1,500-gallons-per-minute pump and 9,000-litre/2,000-gallon water tank.*

■ BELOW *Nevada Division of Forestry runs this distinctively liveried 1989 Spartan GA20/FMC pumper.*

■ BELOW *A 1990 Spartan/Darley foam tender is on duty at the Arco Refinery, Ferndale, Washington. It is operated by Cherry Point Fire and Rescue.*

situations that require long-reach firefighting. This device is especially useful when a foam or water attack is required to be applied at a high, remote or inaccessible level.

GLADIATOR	
Year	1980s
Engine	Series 60 Detroit engine
Power	350–500hp
Transmission	Allison MD-3060P
Features	open cab

■ ABOVE RIGHT *Spartan built this pumper for the Fork Union Fire Company, Fluvanna County, Virginia, USA, in 1993. It carries a 5,700-litres/ 1,250-gallons-per-minute pump.*

■ RIGHT *A 1995 Spartan Silent-Knight/Anderson pumper belonging to Whistler Fire Department, British Columbia, in Canada.*

STEYR-DAIMLER-PUCH

Steyr is one of Austria's main fire engine manufacturers, having for many years built fire vehicles of both heavy and light types. One of the best-known Steyr fire engines is the cross-country all-terrain Pinzgauer series. These rugged models were first introduced in 1971 and developed directly from the smaller 4x4 Haflinger 700AP series that was first produced in 1959. The latter had a rear-mounted, air-cooled, flat twin engine and independent suspension. The larger Pinzgauer features a centre tube chassis that incorporates the 4-speed automatic transmission, and the unitary body frame is then mounted to the chassis tube to provide an exceptionally rigid base. The Pinzgauer comes in 4x4 or 6x6 options, powered by a 5-cylinder, 2.5-litre, turbocharged diesel engine. It is produced for the UK market by Automotive Technik.

Another commonly seen Steyr fire engine includes the Type 4000/220 water tender of the 1970s and 1980s,

PUMPER	
Year	1973
Engine	Ford gas turbine
Power	375hp
Transmission	n/k
Features	experimental vehicle

based on the Steyr 790 4x4 chassis. This had a 170bhp diesel engine, an 18,000-litres/4,000-gallons-per-minute pump, and a 4,000-litre/880-gallon water tank. A number of hydraulic platform and turntable ladders are also mounted on the heavy 1290 series.

Many Steyr fire engines have body-work built by Rosenbauer.

■ ABOVE *This Rosenbauer-bodied Steyr rescue tender is typical of many in operational use with the Austrian Fire Service.*

■ LEFT *A Rosenbauer hydraulic platform, belonging to the fire brigade of the City of Lienz, in the Austrian province of East Tyrol. Traditional Austrian fire helmets are visible through the windscreen.*

SUPERIOR

The Superior Emergency Equipment company of Canada began life in a small plant in Red Deer, Alberta, in 1973 and since then has grown steadily to become Canada's largest manufacturer of fire engines.

Its first fire vehicle, manufactured in 1973, was an industrial pumper built on an International Cargostar tilt-cab chassis. This had a midships-mounted 2,840-litres/625-gallons-per-minute pump. A benchmark in Superior's commercial progress was Calgary Fire Department's order for three pumpers built on a Hendrickson chassis.

■ ABOVE RIGHT *A 1981 Ford C800/Superior pumper of Lovelock Fire Department, Nevada, carries 6,800 litres/1,500 gallons of water and pumps 4,500 litres/1,000 gallons per minute.*

■ BELOW *This 1989 General Motors Corporation/Superior pumper has a roomy crew cab, carries 3,200 litres/700 gallons of water and the pump delivers 4,770 litres/1,050 gallons per minute.*

In the early days, all Superior fire engines were manufactured of steel fabrications, but from 1978 the company began to use all-aluminium construction. In the late 1970s, Superior formed a subsidiary company called Cam-Am Fire Apparatus, Inc, to market Superior fire engines in order to widen sales in north-west America. A number of Superior vehicles were supplied to American fire departments through this company.

A further new division, known as Superior Fire Trucks Ltd, was formed in 1980. Based in Kingston, Ontario, this was primarily to serve Superior users in eastern Canada. Around this time, the parent company entered into an

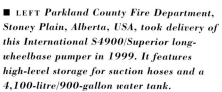

■ LEFT *Parkland County Fire Department, Stoney Plain, Alberta, USA, took delivery of this International S4900/Superior long-wheelbase pumper in 1999. It features high-level storage for suction hoses and a 4,100-litre/900-gallon water tank.*

Then in 1992, Emergency One purchased the Superior Emergency Equipment company and a new firm, Superior Emergency Vehicles, emerged as a subsidiary of Emergency One. Since then, Superior has produced approximately 300 fire engines per year and during 2003 delivered its 3,000th emergency vehicle.

Superior now builds all initial attack and light rescue fire engines for the Emergency One Group. These vehicles include the Wildland units, Grizzly tankers and Lynx mini pumpers on GMC 3500 chassis, and the Super Lynx midi pumpers on the Ford F550 chassis. Light rescue tenders come in various length walk-in units on Ford Super Duty and Medium Duty chassis.

Apart from being Canada's largest builder of domestic fire engines, the Superior Company continues to export various types of fire and rescue vehicles to diverse countries, including Saudi Arabia, Qatar, the Philippines, Colombia, Venezuela, Argentina, Belgium and the Netherlands.

agreement with the American manufacturer of hydraulic platforms, Simon Snorkel, to build this equipment on Superior chassis, but the real springboard for the years ahead came in the mid-1980s with the demise of the large Canadian fire engine builders, Pierreville and King Seagrave. From then on, the commercial fortunes of the company continued apace. In 1987 there were separate agreements with Pierce, Snorkel and Smeal for Superior to have exclusive marketing rights for these makes of fire engine in Canada.

■ ABOVE LEFT *This 1994 Spartan/ Superior 6x4 pumper delivers 4,770 litres/1,050 gallons per minute. The ample bodywork conceals a 7,500-litre/ 1,650-gallon water tank and plenty of stowage.*

■ LEFT *This International 4300/Superior pumper went new in 2002 to Mnjikaning Fire and Rescue, Ontario, Canada.*

SUTPHEN

■ BOTTOM *A 1999 Sutphen long-wheelbase rescue tender of Dagsborough Fire Department, Delaware.*

■ TOP *Jefferson Fire Department, Pennsylvania, run this 1986 Sutphen Deluge pumper.*

The Sutphen Corporation is an old family-owned organization with a very long association with firefighting. Its founder, C H Sutphen, built his first steam fire pump back in 1890 in Columbus, Ohio. Sutphen's son Harry later took his place in the business and grandsons Thomas and Robert joined after World War II. The fifth generation of the family are now making their way through the business, making the more than 110 years of continuous operation unique in fire truck manufacture.

Since those early days, when the first fire engine was built in the garage of one of its employees, the Sutphen corporation has produced a large number of custom-built pumpers at its Ohio headquarters. The corporation has four factories, specializing in different types of trucks. The first manufactures aerial platforms and aluminium pumpers; the second takes orders for boom aerials, platforms and climbing ladders with stainless steel bodies. The third plant assembles the components on the custom chassis, and the last plant manufactures stainless steel and aluminium pumpers for sale throughout the north-east USA. Repair and refurbishment are carried out at two of the plants.

It is probably best known for its front and midship-mounted, telescoping aerial tower ladders. These models use a box-style trussed construction for building an aerial ladder of great strength. Combined with two sets of outrigged jacks, with a total overall spread of 4.5m/15ft, this construction provides maximum stability while the fire engine is working in an elevated and extended position on the fireground.

Apart from dedicated high-rise fire engines, Sutphen also builds a large number of combination firefighting vehicles. These are aerial ladders mounted on a suitable pumper base to allow the fire engine to either pump firefighting water or operate at upper floor level, or both.

OTHER MAKES

SAURER

The Saurer firm, one of the longest-established Swiss manufacturers of commercial trucks, has supplied chassis for many of the country's heavier fire engines, including water tenders, airport foam/crash tenders and turntable ladders. Besides building fire engines for Swiss fire brigades, Saurer also export fire vehicles to Austria and other neighbouring European countries.

Some of the earliest Saurer fire engines were built in 1914 with wooden 18m/60ft Magirus turntable ladders, one of which remained in operational service until 1964. After World War II, the 2DM Saurer 4x4 chassis with a 160bhp diesel engine was used for many standard-pattern Swiss water tenders. These had a rear-mounted pump and a 2,000-litre/440-gallon water tank. In 1958 Saurer delivered a 50m/165ft Magirus turntable ladder to Vienna Fire Service. One of the highest in Europe at the time, this Saurer/Magirus turntable ladder used the 8G-2HL 4x2 chassis powered by a 180bhp V8 diesel engine.

SILSBY

The Silsby Manufacturing Company was formed in 1845 to build steam fire engines for the increasing number of US fire departments. Like a number of fire engine companies, Silsby made its base at Seneca Falls, in New York State, and was soon supplying steam pumps to fire departments from coast to coast. In 1891 Silsby became one of the principal constituents of the American Fire Engine Company, which in 1903 evolved into American LaFrance.

SILVANI

Since its foundation in 1938, Silvani Anticendi has become a major manufacturer of fire engines along with a wide range of other firefighting and fire-protection equipment. Based in Bareggio, Milan, Italy, the Silvani product range includes water tenders, foam tenders and dry-powder units for specialized industrial fire risks, including some heavy vehicles on 6x6 chassis.

Silvani also builds trailer-mounted large-capacity water and foam monitors. Other important features of the Silvani product range are its maritime pump and water fittings for firefighting tugs, and its modular firefighting airborne system for aircraft and helicopters, which are used in aerial attacks on wildland and forest fires.

SKODA

In 1925 this Czechoslovakian car and van manufacturer merged with its rival Laurin and Klement and went on to produce a number of commercial truck chassis, which have been used for fire engines across East Europe. Skoda is now based at Mnichovo Bradiste in the Czech Republic.

Typical Skoda fire engines have included the compact light water tender based on the DVS12L/A Skoda light van chassis with a 1.2-litre, 50bhp engine. This had a crew complement of four firefighters and carried a light portable pump and hose. Skoda also produced a number of ASC25 water tenders using the 706 RTHP 4x4 chassis. This heavier vehicle has a 6-cylinder, 160bhp diesel engine, carries a crew of eight and has a 3,500-litre/770-gallon water tank and carries 200 litres/44 gallons of foam compound. The Skoda 706RTHP water tender has a 2,500-litres/550-gallons-per-minute fire pump. The RTHP chassis is also used for turntable ladders and platforms up to 30m/100ft high. Many Skoda fire engines have bodywork built by the Czech Korosa company.

STAR

For many years fire engines built on the Polish-manufactured Star chassis formed a large part of the pumping vehicles used by Poland's firefighters. The Star water tender, built on the A-26P 4x4 chassis, had a 2,000-litre/440-gallon water tank and carried 120 litres/26 gallons of foam to provide a first-aid foam firefighting attack. A portable pump was carried in addition to the fire engine's integral fire pump.

Some Star military-type chassis were also utilized for fire service use. A number of the 660 6x6 all-terrain chassis, for instance, were used for all-terrain emergency tenders. In the late 1970s Star was one the first East European fire engine builders to incorporate the use of alloy roller shutters for equipment lockers into its water tender design.

STONEFIELD

The short-lived British Stonefield Vehicles Ltd manufactured a number of fire engines in both 4x4 and 6x4 configurations that were unusual for their chassis-less construction. From 1978 six Stonefield emergency tenders, powered by 5.2-litre V8 petrol engines with an automatic gearbox, went into service with English and Scottish fire brigades. Others were supplied to airport fire brigades.

■ BELOW *A Stonefield P5000 emergency tender.*

TATRA

Tatra started manufacturing cars in Kopprivnice, now in the Czech Republic, in 1919 and since then has also been a principal supplier of chassis for fire engines, many being delivered to other East European countries, including Poland and former East Germany. Many vehicles have bodywork fitted by Korosa, another Czech company. The

■ ABOVE RIGHT *This Tatra 6x4/Bronto 40m/131ft hydraulic platform is in service with Prague Fire Brigade.*

■ RIGHT *A 6x4 Tatra rescue tender of Prague Fire Brigade.*

Tatra 138 and the later 148 6x6 series were typical heavy chassis used for foam tenders. These incorporated a six-man crew cab, a 3,000-litres/660-gallons-per-minute pump, a 6,000-litre/1,320-gallon water tank, and a 600-litre/132-gallon foam tank. These Tatra chassis were also used for turntable ladders, usually of Metz or Magirus origin.

THIBAULT

The Thibault name is synonymous with Canadian-built fire engines. The company originated in the early twentieth century, when its founder, Charles Thibault, first built manual pumps, then horse-drawn fire engines, before completing his first motor fire engine, a Ford, in 1918.

Charles's son, Pierre, assumed command of the developing business in 1938 when the company relocated to Pierreville, Quebec. Throughout World War II, Thibault produced a range of government firefighting vehicles and equipment, but at the end of hostilities,

■ LEFT *This Shell-owned 1956 Ford F/Thibault foam tender served at Shellburn Refinery No.1, Burnaby, in British Columbia. It carried 3,800 litres/840 gallons of foam concentrate.*

returned to building fire engines for Canada's fire departments.

Supplying both pumpers on custom chassis and, from 1960, aerials, Thibault went from strength to strength. Its aerials were particularly successful, with many ladder sections being supplied to American fire engine manufacturers for incorporation into their own products. By then, Thibault fire engines were in widespread operational use across Canada and export orders were delivered to fire brigades in the West Indies and South America.

When the founder's grandsons started their own independent fire engine manufacturing operation under the Pierreville name in 1968, Thibault began to suffer commercially, and was declared bankrupt in 1972. It was sold on, only to suffer the same fate again five years later. The Thibault name eventually re-emerged as Camions Pierre Thibault, Inc.

When the nearby Pierreville operation closed down in 1985, most of the company assets were assumed under the Thibault name before Camions Pierre

LIGHT PUMPER	
Year	1975
Engine	V6 petrol
Power	6-litre
Transmission	5-speed manual
Features	4x4

Thibault, Inc, went bankrupt in 1990. A new Canadian company, Nova Quintech Corporation, acquired the Thibault assets and continued the manufacture of pumpers and aerials. In 1995, however, it decided to concentrate its activities on aerial fire engines, and two years later the American fire engine company Pierce acquired the Nova Quintech aerial ladder business.

The Thibault family link with the world of fire engines was maintained by several family members who continued their various business interests in Canada, building pumpers and tankers, and other items of firefighting and rescue equipment.

■ ABOVE *A Thibault utility lighting vehicle with open rear cab of Neptune Rose Fire Company, Burlington, New Jersey, USA.*

THORNYCROFT

The Thornycroft chassis were first used for fire engines in the 1930s, but the company's name is probably better remembered for its airport and airfield crash tenders, built in considerable numbers in the 1950s and 1960s.

Based at Basingstoke, England, the company supplied 4x4 and 6x4 Nubian variants for military and civil use. With roof-mounted foam monitor jets, the Nubians were fitted with either the Rolls-Royce B80 or B81 5.7-litre, 8-cylinder petrol engines developing 140bhp, giving a Nubian a top speed of 95kmh/60mph. These airport tenders weighed in at 14 tons, but with ever-larger passenger jets, the demand for greater aviation firefighting capacity continued to increase, so in 1964

■ RIGHT *A c.1970 Thornycroft Nubian Major/Dennis Mk 9 6x4 crash tender originally supplied to the British Royal Air Force Fire and Rescue Service.*

Thornycroft introduced the Nubian Major. This much more powerful 6x6 aviation fire engine was powered by a V8 Cummins diesel engine with 300bhp through a 5-speed semi-automatic

gearbox. This gave it a creditable performance of reaching 65kmh/40mph in 41 seconds. Firefighting foam output was rated at 31,800 litres/7,000 gallons per minute.

NUBIAN MAJOR 6X4 (20-TON)	
Year	1966
Engine	V8 diesel
Power	300bhp
Transmission	5-speed semi-automatic
Features	66kmh/41mph in 41 secs

■ LEFT *A Thornycroft Nubian Major/HCB Angus 6x4 foam tender in service at Dubai International Airport, in the United Arab Emirates.*

TOYNE

Toyne is an American manufacturer based in Breda, Iowa. It was here that in 1942 founder Gilbert Toyne built his first fire engine body based on a Model T Ford for a local fire department. Toyne expanded his fire engine business, delivering front-mounted pumpers equiped with 2,270-litre/500-gallon water tanks. The company steadily built up a well-founded reputation for quality and heavy-duty construction, especially in off-road rural firefighting.

In 2001, Toyne doubled the size of its engineering department, and today manufactures a wide range of pumpers, rescue pumpers, tankers and aerials, with bodies constructed of heavy-duty aluminium, stainless steel or Toyne's exclusive bolted/brushed stainless steel design. The pumpers can be customized or commercial, and include the Metrocat heavy-duty aluminium body, severe-duty custom chassis, or polished unpainted stainless steel.

The tanker range includes heavy-duty vehicles with varying capacities (4,500–15,900 litres/1,000–3,500 gallons) and front or midship-mounted pumps, or portables. Aerial ladders include a selection of 15–33.2m/50–109ft rear-mount types along with 23m/75ft and 31.7m/104ft mid-mount platforms. These aerials are available in a choice of formed stainless steel, aluminium or bolted/brushed stainless steel construction.

TOYOTA

The Tokyo-based Japanese car manufacturer Toyota has built a large number of chassis suitable for fire engine use. These have included many with bodies (pumps, aerial ladders and platforms) built by Morita, another Japanese company. In the early 1960s, Toyota still produced an open-bodied pump for urban Japanese fire brigades. This was based on the FC80 chassis that was powered by a six-cylinder petrol engine of 145bhp with four-speed manual gearbox.

Toyota chassis are particularly used for the MWG 40T pump, which incorporates a 2,270 litres/500 gallons per minute water pump, a 4,000-litre/880-gallon water tank and a crew

BJ 4x4	
Year	1955
Engine	6-cylinder petrol
Power	3.3-litre
Transmission	manual
Features	all-terrain light pump

cab that accommodates six firefighters. This model has been exported to fire brigades in Asia and the Far East. Toyota also build a 4x4 chassis suitable for a compact six-crew water tender designed for working within the confines of the narrow streets typical of many older Japanese cities.

■ ABOVE *A c.1980 Toyota Dyna control unit of the Delhi Fire Service, India, carries a folded telescopic radio aerial on the roof. The red and white chequered markings are traditionally used to identify the central control point at a fire. Usually, they are applied to the upper half of a vehicle, but in this case no half measures have been taken.*

OTHER MAKES

■ TEMAX

Founded in 1965, Temax SA is the major manufacturer of fire engines in Greece. The company operates from its Athens production base, building a range of firefighting and rescue vehicles for Greek fire brigades, the armed forces, the civil aviation authority, the forestry departments and several industrial companies.

Many Temax fire engines are built on commercial chassis, including Chrysler, Mercedes-Benz, Scania, and Volvo. Temax pumpers are available with pumping capacities varying from 400 litres/88 gallons per minute to 6,000 litres/1,320 gallons per minute, and water tank capacity options from 500–12,000 litres/110–2,640 gallons.

The Temax range of firefighting tenders can be configured according to a fire brigade's precise needs. Some of the options available for airport fire tenders include manual or remote-controlled roof-mounted monitors, manual or automatic foam systems, ground-sweep nozzles, remote-control facilities, and manual or electric-rewind hose reels.

VARLEY

Varley Specialised Vehicles was formed in 1999 as an offshoot of the Australian parent company, Warley, which is involved in manufacturing, defence, power, and ship repair activities.

The new division was formed with the intention of building fire engines utilizing special-purpose components, Rosenbauer pumping technology and Magirus firefighting equipment. Two

■ LEFT *In 2000, Queensland Fire and Rescue Service, Australia, bought this Varley urban pumper built on a Scania 94D 310 chassis.*

TYPE 5 COMMANDER	
Year	2002
Engine	6-cylinder diesel
Power	274bhp
Transmission	automatic
Features	urban pumper

mainstream designs were developed – the Trident airport crash tender and the Firepac pumper. Both these models have drawn on combined bus and coach chassis manufacture and are in widespread use throughout Australian fire brigades.

The Firepac 4-door urban pumper has greater crew cab space than normal, together with a tilt cab that gives excellent access to the Caterpillar 250hp diesel power unit. The unique

cab design of the Firepac provides rollover protection and allows easy exit from and access to the cab for a crew, especially when wearing breathing sets.

This Firepac also has a ZF 5-speed automatic transmission and air-bag suspension on both front and rear axles. A Rosenbauer NH30 pump provides a maximum pumping performance of 3,000 litres/660 gallons per minute, and there is a choice of tank capacity options, from 1,000–2,000 litres/220–440 gallons.

VOLKAN

■ BELOW *A Turkish Fire Service Ford/Volkan pump with 15m/50ft turntable ladder.*

Based in Izmir, Turkey, Volkan has been manufacturing fire engines since 1974, offering a bodybuilding design and supply service for urban, rural, airport, petrochemical and industrial fire brigades vehicles. The range includes water tenders, pumps, foam tenders and turntable ladders using chassis which include Mercedes and IVECO.

FOAM TENDER	
Year	2002
Engine	6-cylinder diesel
Power	326bhp
Transmission	manual
Features	4x4

VOLKSWAGEN

Volkswagen light vehicles have been used for many years by European fire brigades, both as light fire tenders and for the general firefighting and rescue transportation of equipment, including light portable pumps and hose, and for the movement of personnel. The Volkswagen Combi and the LT31 series have been used regularly in various first-aid firefighting roles in support of major fire engines. Volkswagen is based in Wolfsburg, Germany.

■ LEFT *This c.1960 Volkswagen utility vehicle was used as a staff car by Stadt-Bottrop Fire Brigade, Germany.*

VOLVO

Volvo produced its first commercial trucks in 1928, just a year after its first cars rolled off the production line in Gothenburg, Sweden. One of the earliest Volvo fire engines built in that first year used an LV45 chassis and was built for the City of Gothenburg. The demand was such that Volvo started to produce a chassis specifically for fire brigade use.

There then followed a series of Volvo chassis fitted with a 6-cylinder, 4-litre engine. Approximately 1,700 Volvo LV70s with a 4-litre, 6-cylinder engine were built between 1931 and 1936, most of which were used for fire engine or bus applications. The LV70, along with the LV68, was one of the first Volvo truck models to run on fuel other than petrol, when the Hesselman engine,

which was able to run on several different fuels including fuel oil, was introduced in 1933. Volvo used this engine from 1933 until 1947 when it completed the design of its first diesel engine.

■ ABOVE *In 1928 the first Volvo truck to be used as a fire engine had a 28hp 2-litre petrol engine. It carried rolled hose.*

■ BELOW *By the 1930s the Volvo LV90 fire engine boasted a front-mounted pump and wheeled 15m/50ft escape ladder.*

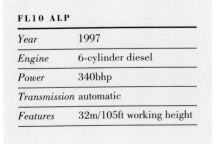

FL10 ALP	
Year	1997
Engine	6-cylinder diesel
Power	340bhp
Transmission	automatic
Features	32m/105ft working height

■ LEFT *A 1988 Volvo FL6 17/Metz 30m/ 100ft turntable ladder on duty with Hampshire Fire Brigade, England.*

■ BELOW LEFT *This Minnesota-based 1987 Volvo N12/Hills 6x4 tanker has a 15,900-litre/3,500-gallon water capacity.*

already taken delivery of six Volvo FL10 8x4 Bronto 33m/109ft aerial ladder platforms. At that time, these were the tallest aerials in service with any UK fire brigade.

In 1992 the FL617 was replaced by the FL618 and joined by a higher-powered alternative, the FS7. This 7-litre diesel-engine version of the well proven FL6 provided an 11 per cent improvement in power and a 33 per cent increase in torque over the most powerful 6-litre unit then standard in the FL6. In 1995 Volvo introduced a new turbocharged 6-litre engine, which had been designed specifically to meet fire brigade demand for a higher-powered, compact engine to boost performance. It produced 19 per cent more power and 18 per cent more torque than the existing engine.

Volvo has developed chassis for specific operating needs. For instance, Hampshire Fire and Rescue Service, in England, has an FL618 with a specially

Outside Scandinavia Volvo initially tailored two models, the FL616 and the FL617, to cover the bulk of its fire applications. The FL614 chassis was introduced primarily for use as a water tender, with the heavier FL617 being used for hydraulic platforms and as a prime mover for demountable bodies. Although Volvo commercial vehicles were available in the UK from 1967, it was not until the FL6 truck series was introduced in the mid-1980s that Volvo fire engines started to appear in the UK. Today, Volvo fire engines are in service in most of the UK's fire brigades.

Volvo's success in the UK firefighting arena is reflected by orders for more than 300 vehicles from over half of Britain's 60 public fire brigades. The first large order for the FL614 came in 1990, when London Fire Brigade, the UK's largest fire authority, requested 34 water tenders. The capital's brigade had

■ BELOW *A 1992 Volvo FL6 14/HCB Angus rescue water tender.*

■ RIGHT *This long-wheelbase Volvo Autocar tanker is operated by Selbyville Fire Department, Delaware.*

low cab height and Metz turntable ladder. The vehicle is 212mm/8¼in lower than standard in order to provide access to the inner courtyard of Winchester Cathedral via a low arch.

Five FL611s, some of the smallest water tenders Volvo has ever supplied in the UK, are currently in service in Cumbria, England, to afford easy travel through the narrow and winding lanes of the region's Lake District. In 1997, a new mobile incident command unit based on the Volvo B6 Midbus chassis went into service in Greater Manchester County Fire Service. It was the first time that this particular chassis had been put to use for duties other than passenger carrying. In 1977, London Fire Brigade commissioned a similar coach-based Volvo/Spectra command unit.

OTHER MAKES

■ VAN PELT/FMC

American fire engine builder Van Pelt started business in 1925 in Oakdale, California. The company built up a customer base on the Pacific coast with a range of custom-built pumpers and aerial ladders.

After World War II, Van Pelt ceased to make its own chassis, offering instead a range of fire engines built upon suitable commercial alternatives such as Duplex, Ford and Spartan. In 1984, the Van Pelt Company was acquired by the FMC (Food Mechanical Corporation), one of the world's largest manufacturers of military and agricultural caterpillar vehicles. At that time, FMC also had a fire engine division originally formed in 1965 by its acquisition of the John Bean Company. This latter manufacturer was one of the pioneers of the use of high-pressure firefighting water pumps for fire engines.

The enlarged company produced the Quick Attacker short-bodied pumper range with various pumping capacities available from 1,125–6,800 litres/250–1,500 gallons per minute. These pumpers also had an impressive 2.43cu m/86cu ft of inboard storage. In addition, the Van Pelt/FMC range included the Roughneck series budget pumper, tankers with capacities of up to 11,300 litres/2,500 gallons and various aerial ladder configurations.

Apart from its fire engines for American operational use, numerous types of Van Pelt/FMC fire engines were built for service in more than 30 countries. The company finally ceased fire vehicle production in 1990 to concentrate on manufacturing aviation equipment.

■ VOGT

Based at Oberdiessbach in Switzerland, VOGT build a range of pumpers, foam tenders and airport crash tenders for the international market. The fire engines are often based on Mercedes and Scania chassis among others with 4x4, 6x4, and 8x4 configurations. Foam tenders are available with multi-compartments for up to four different types of extinguishing media plus a dry powder unit.

■ ABOVE *This 1971 Duplex/Van Pelt was acquired by Ukiah Fire Department, California in 1989 from Redwood City.*

The company is noted for its use of electronic pump controls. VOGT fire engines can be fitted with a programmable logic controller that has complete control of the vehicle's water pump delivery, up to 6,000 litres/1,320 gallons per minute. Hose lines and outlets are operated via electro-pneumatic valves, which monitor water pressures to ensure that maximum operating levels are not exceeded. Precise amounts of foam concentrate can also be controlled. This system allows the firefighter at the hose branch to control the settings of water and foam as well as to operate the pump via a radio link.

WARD LAFRANCE

■ BELOW *Los Angeles County Fire Department, Pearblossom, California, took delivery of this new Ward LaFrance Ambassador pumper in 1972. It has a 4,500-litres/1,000-gallons-per-minute pump and 2,270-litre/500-gallon water tank.*

The Ward LaFrance fire engine company was founded in Elmira Heights, New York, in 1918 by A Ward LaFrance, who soon became a principal force in the American firefighting equipment industry. It has no connection with American LaFrance, which was founded earlier by another family member.

The company produced large numbers of fire engines leading up to World War II, and in 1937 introduced a restyled range of open-cab bonneted pumpers with midships-mounted pumps and incorporating a fire crew standing area in the rear body. These designs contributed to the developing shape and design of American fire engines of that time.

Ward LaFrance continued to produce the Fireball pumper range in the 1950s, following it with the 1960s Fire Brand models. A further new arrival in the range was the P80 Ambassador pumper, which was powered by a 6-cylinder Waukesha F817G petrol engine with 280bhp and a 5-speed manual gearbox. Offered as part of this new pumper in 1968 was the Ward LaFrance command tower – a vehicle-width, 6.7m/22ft elevating platform, raised by hydraulic rams. Fitted with a vertical access ladder, the tower carried a 4,500-litre/1,000-gallon monitor and could be used as a lighting platform or aerial command control point.

Ward LaFrance also produced a number of 23–30m/75–100ft aerial ladders, both rear and midships-mounted, together with hydraulic platforms up to 26m/85ft. All these aerials were available on two or tandem-axle chassis, depending on weight factors. The company has also built several compact pumpers and other fire engines, together with a number of telescopic-boomed water towers, on 4x4 chassis, such as the International range.

■ ABOVE *A 1973 Ward LaFrance pumper of Orbisonia-Rockhill Fire Department, Pennsylvania.*

■ BELOW *A 1976 International 2010A Ward LaFrance pumper with a 4,500-litre/1,000-gallon water tank and pump.*

WESTATES

In 1956 the Westates Truck Body Company began trading in Redwood City, California. After building a number of commercial truck bodies, Westates began to manufacture fire engine bodies for the California State Division of Forestry. During the early 1960s, the company delivered its first heavy rescue unit and from then on Westates regularly built fire engines for many American municipal fire departments.

Westates relocated to new premises in Menlo Park, California, in 1969 and in 1983 moved to its present location at Woodland, California.

In 1977, Westates designed the original through-the-tank ladder tunnel arrangement, and the company continued its strong technological leadership. In 1996 an industrial

■ ABOVE *A 1985 Ford L8000/ Westates pumper of Snohomish County Fire District, Getchell, Washington.*

■ LEFT *A1984 Duplex D350/ Westates pumper based in Antloch, California.*

■ LEFT *Skagit County Fire District, LaConner, Washington, operate this 1983 Ford C/Westates pumper with a 4,500-litres/ 1,000-gallons-per-minute pump and a similar capacity water tank.*

PUMPER

Year	1986
Engine	6-cylinder diesel
Power	350bhp
Transmission manual	
Features	6,810lpm/1,500gpm pump

laser-cutting machine, which worked to European standards, was installed at the premises, and one year later, a laser-cut stainless steel fire engine body became a Westates standard.

Today, the Westates L2000 series uses a modular bodywork design and is available on all the company's range of pumpers, rescue tenders and aerial ladders.

■ LEFT *A 1986 International S2674 chassis provides the base for this Westates 6,800-litres/1,500-gallons-per-minute pumper with a 3,400-litre/750-gallon water tank.*

WESTERN STATES

This American fire apparatus company started life as the Neep Fire Equipment of Cornelius, Oregon. Neep sold firefighting equipment and developed this work into the building of their first fire engine in 1941. This was followed by a number of other fire department vehicles and in the 1940s, Gloyd Hall acquired the interests of the Neep company and the brand name was changed to Western States Fire Apparatus, Inc.

Trading under this new title, the company continued its steady output of fire engines, building mostly a range of pumpers, including front-mounted, midships, and Intra-Cab models, and various other types of pumper tenders.

To date, over 1,200 separate Western States fire engines have been delivered to fire departments throughout the American north-west, and in Texas, California, Colorado and Wyoming. Some Western States pumpers have also been exported to Kuwait.

■ ABOVE RIGHT *Front-mounted pump controls and inlets/outlets are a feature of this 1975 Seagrave/Western States 6x4 pumper.*

■ RIGHT *Portland Fire Bureau, Oregon, operate this 1981 Spartan pumper with a typical Western States front-mounted pump.*

■ ABOVE *A 1962 Ford F800/Western States light pumper of Skagit County Fire District, Birdsview, Washington.*

WHITE

The White brothers, Thomas, Rollin, Walter and Windsor built their first steam engine in 1900, building on the success of their father's sewing machine business. Productivity increased year on year, and the range of vehicles expanded to include buses, police patrol wagons, fire apparatus and later, sightseeing buses. Petrol-powered engines made their first appearance in 1909 and in 1916 the company was reorganized under the name White Motor Company. The company merged with Freightliner Trucks after having acquired Sterling in 1951 and Autocar in 1953. By 1975 the newly named White Truck Group had also acquired Diamon Reo, but by 1981 the company was bankrupt and bought out, and it disappeared in 1995.

■ ABOVE *A 1991 White/General Motors/Anderson pumper in British Columbia.*

■ LEFT *A 1990 rescue unit based on a White/General Motors/Autocar/ Computerlog arrangement.*

■ LEFT *Used to deal with spillages and leakages of toxic chemicals, this hazardous material unit of Reno Fire Department, Nevada, is built on a 1986 White/Marion chassis.*

LIGHT PUMPER

Year	1975
Engine	V6 petrol
Power	6-litre
Transmission	5-speed manual
Features	4x4

OTHER MAKES

■ WATEROUS

The Waterous Company was founded in St Paul, Minnesota, USA, in 1886 by the two Waterous brothers, to manufacture horse-drawn steam fire engines and other firefighting equipment. Waterous fire engines were soon in use across America and in 1898 the company had pioneered a petrol-driven water pump pulled by horses. In 1906 Waterous produced a petrol-powered pumper with separate engines for road traction and water-pump power. One year later it produced a pumper that used a single petrol engine for both road propulsion and pump power. Waterous ceased to build complete fire engines in 1929 in order to concentrate on developing firefighting water-pump technology, which it offered to other fire engine builders worldwide. Today Waterous fire pumps are the most frequently specified types in North America, and a number are in operational service around the world.

■ WAWRZASZEK

The Wawrzaszek Special Engineering Company, based in Bielsko-Biala, Poland, builds a varied range of firefighting and rescue vehicles. These include pumps and aerial ladders and platforms, hazardous material incident units and support vehicles for a variety of high-risk fire protection industries. Suitable commercial chassis are used according to payload and specification.

YOUNG

Allen Case founded his American fire
engine-building company in 1932.
It was known as Cayasler before it
assumed the title of Young Fire
Equipment Company in 1944. Until it
ceased trading in 1991, Young built over
2,000 fire engines at its production
plants around Buffalo, New York State.
In later years it produced 22.5m/
73ft 8in hydraulic platforms built on the
Young Crusader chassis, and a number
of pumpers were built with folding rear
crew-cab doors operated by a
compressed-air mechanism.

■ ABOVE *Mt Jackson Fire Department,
Shenandoah County, Virginia, operates this
1989 Young Crusader II pumper, which
incorporates a roomy rear crew cab*
*compartment. The mid-mounted pump has a
capacity of 5,700 litres/1,250 gallons per
minute, while the water tank holds 2,270
litres/500 gallons.*

ZIEGLER

■ BELOW *A 2002 MAN/Ziegler 8x8 airport
foam tender at Stuttgart Airport, Germany.*

Albert Ziegler founded his hose-
manufacturing company in 1890 in
Giengen, Germany, and although it
steadily expanded its range of
firefighting equipment, it did not build
a fire engine until 1953. The first was a
KFL6 water tender constructed on an
Opel Lightning 1.75-ton chassis. From

then on, a range of Ziegler engine types
were developed, using diesel engines for
the first time in 1963. Some of the early
vehicles went to European brigades.

In 1969 Ziegler's first airport crash
tender went into service in Copenhagen.
By this time the company was supplying
an ever-expanding range of water

tenders, rescue tenders, aerial ladders,
airport foam/crash tenders and other
firefighting vehicles, as well as
continuing to develop its fire pump and
equipment side of the business.

Today, Ziegler is Germany's largest
firefighting equipment manufacturer and
supplies very large numbers of fire

engines and components to fire brigades in over 70 countries. Current Ziegler fire vehicles range from the small VRW quick-response light rescue vehicles, to the huge 8x8 FLF 60/Z8 airport foam tender. The Ziegler VRW is based on various commercial chassis, including the Mercedes-Benz 412D 4x2 with a 5-cylinder 122 bhp engine, and the Chevrolet Suburban K 2500 4x4 with a V8 engine with 250bhp. It is equipped either with a light water unit or a complement of rescue tools and electrical power.

At the other end of the Ziegler range is the FLF 60 Z8 airport foam tender, which weighs just over 38 tons and carries a crew of three. This uses a MAN 38.1000 8x8 chassis with a 12-cylinder, 1,000bhp engine with automatic transmission, which provides a 0–80kmh/50mph performance in approximately 20 seconds. The FLF 60 Z8 carries 12,000 litres/2,666 gallons of water, 1,500 litres/330 gallons of foam concentrate, and 500kg/1100lb of dry powder. The Ziegler fire pump has a maximum output of 7,000 litres/1,540 gallons per minute, the roof-mounted monitor delivers 5,000 litres/1,100 gallons per minute and 1,000 litres/ 220 gallons are delivered through the front-mounted monitor. Both monitors are remotely controlled from the driving cab.

Ziegler also supplies the DLK 23/12 turntable ladder on the Mercedes Benz Atego 1528 or the MAN 15.264 chassis, and the Bronto Skylift F32 MDT aerial platform ladder on the Mercedes Benz Atego1828 or MAN 18.264 chassis.

VLF 24/12

Year	2002
Engine	6-cylinder diesel
Power	240hp
Transmission	automatic or manual
Features	quick-response pumper

■ ABOVE LEFT *This 2002 MAN 14.254/Ziegler TLF 16/25 4x4 water tender was built for the German Fire Service.*

■ ABOVE RIGHT *A c.1970 Opel Blitz/Ziegler rescue tender of the Bad Nauheim Fire Brigade, Germany.*

■ LEFT *Lüdenscheid Fire Brigade, Germany, use Ziegler-bodied fire engines, such as this Mercedes 1019/Ziegler rescue tender.*

OTHER MAKES

■ ZIL

From 1942 onwards the UAZ Moscow truck and van factory built a number of small first-aid fire engines for Russian fire brigades, using the UAZ 450A 4x4 van chassis. After 1956, however, all standard Russian-built fire engines were constructed under the ZIL badge and a vast number of ZIL fire engines went into service right across the Soviet bloc. These included the ZIL 130 and 150 series 4x2 water tenders of the late 1950s, which were powered by a 6-cylinder, 95bhp engine. Both series had a 1,800 litres/400 gallons per minute pump, but the ZIL 130 had a

2,100-litre/460-gallon water tank, while the 150 series had the slightly larger 2,150-litre/470-gallon version. Some ZIL 130 models also included a 500-litre/ 110-gallon foam concentrate tank to provide a firefighting attack at oil refineries and petrochemical plants.

ZIL also produced a special heavy chassis known as the 131 6x6 series, designed for a Soviet-manufactured AL-30 30m/100ft turntable ladder.

ZIL water tenders and turntable ladders have found their way to a number of countries outside the former Soviet Union, including Iran and Egypt, as well as several African countries.

INDEX